INTERNATIONAL PAPER

South Carolina's
PLANTATIONS & HISTORIC HOMES

South Carolina's
PLANTATIONS & HISTORIC HOMES

Paul M. Franklin and Nancy Mikula

Voyageur Press

ACKNOWLEDGMENTS

We would like to express our deepest thanks to the many members of South Carolina's tourism offices and various historical preservation societies for assisting us in identifying, researching, and gaining access to the homes in this book. In particular we would like to thank Amy Ballenger-Guest of the Charleston Area Convention and Visitors Bureau and Carol Anne Bowers of the Historic Charleston Foundation, who made the impossible possible; Dawn Dawson-House of the South Carolina Department of Parks, Recreation and Tourism for being our gracious host in so many places; and Jim Wescott of Lowcountry Tourism, Barbara Ware of Old 96 District, and Freddie Marshal Neel, provider of Edgefield historical tours, who located houses and histories that were all but forgotten. Finally, thanks to our new friend, Jayne Scarborough of the Olde English District, who opened doors for us and introduced us to the beauty and warmth of South Carolina's heartland.

First published in 2006 by Voyageur Press, an imprint of MBI Publishing Company, Galtier Plaza, Suite 200, 380 Jackson Street, St. Paul, MN 55101-3885 USA

ON THE TITLE PAGE: JOSEPH MANIGAULT HOUSE, STAIRCASE **FACING PAGE:** THE RHETT HOUSE

MBI Publishing Company titles are also available at discounts in bulk quantity for industrial or sales-promotional use. For details write to Special Sales Manager at MBI Publishing Company, Galtier Plaza, Suite 200, 380 Jackson Street, St. Paul, MN 55101-3885 USA

ISBN-13: 978-0-7603-2540-7
ISBN-10: 0-7603-2540-5

Editor: Michael Dregni
Designer: Julie Vermeer

Printed in China

CONTENTS

OPPOSITE PAGE: JOSEPH MANIGAULT HOUSE SEEN THROUGH ITS GATEHOUSE.

Introduction

SOUTH CAROLINA'S PLANTATIONS
& HISTORIC HOMES

Houses are the most honest historians. Built by real people to meet the needs of their time, they tell the stories of lives lived and lost, of children born and raised. They bear the very real marks of economic success and failure, and they reflect the hopes and dreams of their builders. Plain or gilded, they are shelters in which families live and grow; and in their bricks, boards, and mortar live the ghosts of joy and laughter, sorrow and tears.

In the eighteenth and nineteenth centuries, the plantations of South Carolina created wealth on a level the world has rarely seen. South Carolina planters built family empires whose riches rivaled or exceeded those of the aristocratic planters of Virginia and the great shipping and mercantile families of New England. These families celebrated their wealth in the lives they lived. They traveled to Europe to collect great works of art and educated their children in England's finest schools. At home, they created a unique world of social elegance and courtly behavior that borrowed its formality from European high society and blended it with the warm manners and hospitality of Colonial America. Today, nowhere is the world of the antebellum planter more alive than within the walls of the houses they built.

The very words "southern plantation" elicit visions of grace and grandeur, of elegant homes with graceful white columns, and of carriage rides along lanes shaded by rows of fragrant magnolias or moss-draped live oaks. Yet not all plantation homes were grand and opulent. Some were simple farmhouses, built with hand tools and hard labor to shelter the planter's family. Others are stately symbols of affluence that reflect the reserved tastes of England and continental Europe. Yet others, particularly those built in the closing decades of the antebellum era, are romantic and fanciful displays of the wealth created during booming years of "King Cotton." Rich or poor, simple or opulent, all plantations shared the risks and hardships of the day. Every year, success and disaster were determined by the weather and the quality of harvests; all faced the trials of wars, natural disasters, and periods of economic upheaval.

These houses tell much about the history of South Carolina and the United States through the stories of the people who built and lived in them. They bring the past alive, allowing us to walk floors that were trod by Robert E. Lee, to sit on a porch where George Washington took tea, or to stand in the room where Jefferson Davis finally accepted that his beloved way of life had ended. Step into the ballroom at Hampton Plantation, and it is suddenly easier to hear the music of violins and the clink of wine glasses and to envision elegantly dressed men and women dancing beneath the lights of the glittering chandeliers.

MAGNOLIA PLANTATION

The First Planters

In the seventeenth century, both France and Spain made attempts to settle on the coast of South Carolina, but it was the English who came and stayed. King Charles II, wishing to reward those who supported him in the restoration of the monarchy, designated eight Lords Proprietors to whom he gave the right to develop and profit from the Carolinas. They in turn solicited hardy men and women to found settlements in the raw new land. The first of these settlers arrived in 1670, initially settling at Albemarle Point on the Ashley River, but eventually relocating to found Charles Town, the present-day Charleston. The fortified settlement they built there became one of three medieval-style walled cities in North America. (The others were France's Québec and Spain's St. Augustine).

The settlers soon began establishing plantations along the fertile banks of the Ashley and Cooper rivers. These first settlers lived in primitive homes and the first products of their plantations were the raw materials at hand: timber, deer skins, wild game, and turpentine and pine pitch for the Royal Navy.

Freedom of religion was one of the founding philosophies of the Carolina Colony and the first waves of immigrants included Protestant Scots and French Huguenots. But it was settlers from the West Indies who set the tone for the culture of South Carolina's coastal Low Country. The West Indies had been a haven for English adventurers, and many Barbadians, as they were called, had developed vastly wealthy sugar plantations; by the 1680s, however, there was little land left, and a series of natural disasters forced many to seek new horizons in the newly created Carolina Colony.

These Barbadians arrived with two things that were in huge demand in the Carolinas—wealth and experience turning raw land into more wealth. They made their wealth with three crops. Sugar was the first, but it proved unsuited to the climate. The other two—rice and indigo—thrived in the marshy land beyond all expectations. These crops were incredibly labor intensive, but the Barbadians had a solution to that problem: They brought along large numbers of African slaves as well as an established slave trade that was highly organized and breathtakingly profitable.

The Barbadians also carried to the Low Country their love of elegant social functions and the good life. As strictly religious Protestant cultures began settling in the Up Country, the Barbadians did little more than tip their hat to the church. It was the beginning of the division of South Carolina into its two strong cultures: the freewheeling Barbadian-influenced culture of the Low Country with its emphasis on beauty, pleasure, and practical politics; and the reserved Up Country with its strong religious base, which shunned extravagant living and blatant displays of wealth.

South Carolina Architectural Styles and Influences

Plantations were far more than houses. Throughout their history, they were self-sufficient social and economic centers. The plantation had to provide most of the food, clothing, shelter, tools, and entertainment for the owner's family as well as for an extensive population of house servants, craftsmen, field supervisors, and often three hundred or more field slaves. Entertaining visitors was also a major part of plantation life, and the plantation owner was obliged to offer hospitality—sometimes for weeks at a time—to his guests.

Many plantation houses featured flankers, which usually were detached wings, located symmetrically on each side of the main house. Flankers contained service spaces and guest lodging. Behind the house would be a detached kitchen where the day-long job of feeding the planter's family, guests, and house servants took place. The kitchen was located behind the house because of fear of fire and to reduce heat buildup in the main house during the humid summer months. Farther away from the house would be a spring house for cooling dairy products, a smokehouse, stables, and often a blacksmith shop. During an average day, the plantation grounds were a beehive of activity; wagons and horses went to and from the fields, and a small army of servants hauled water, did laundry, tended the house gardens, and fed horses and livestock.

As immigrants—including increasing numbers of Huguenots, Scots, and transplants from Virginia and North Carolina—continued to flood into South Carolina, they began to settle in the wilderness of the Up Country. The houses they built were solid and functional. Some, such as Paul de St. Julien's elegant little Hanover House, built in 1716, served not only as shelter, but also as fortresses—and not without cause. In 1715, an alliance of native tribes led by the Yemassee, fed up with poor treatment from the colonials, staged a bloody uprising, burning scores of plantations and killing more than one hundred settlers.

By 1740, Charleston had entered its golden era. The city docks were crowded with ships transporting rice and indigo to Europe and importing fine furniture, porcelain, spices, and other necessities and luxuries. As the planters became affluent, then wealthy, they built larger, fancier houses. Many of these planters had been born and educated in England. Little wonder then, that they modeled their grand new homes after the classic Georgian style of architecture found on English country estates. Georgian architecture celebrates symmetry and balance, and many of its details, such as large, arched windows and fan-shaped windows (or "lights") over doorways are Palladian in origin, from the sixteenth-century designs of Andrea Palladio.

Many planters chose to build second "townhouses" in Charleston, Beaufort, or Columbia to enjoy the refinements of city life. Often these homes were more ornate showplaces than the plantation homes. Some owners rarely returned to their plantations, preferring to leave the work of planting and harvest to overseers. Other planters fled the Low Country in summer to avoid malaria and other fevers, believed to come from "marsh vapors" liberated by the summer heat. Towns such as Walterboro, chosen for its relatively high elevation, became summer communities for these wealthy families. Many

of these summer homes (as well as some working plantations like The Grove on Edisto Island) were built high off the ground to avoid the vapors. This elevated building style was fortuitous, as scientists later proved the female mosquito that carries malaria rarely flies more than a few feet above ground.

PREVIOUS PAGES: BOONE HALL PLANTATION

South Carolina played an important role in the Revolutionary War. Regional militias led by such men as Francis Marion (whose exploits Hollywood would document more than two hundred years later in the Mel Gibson movie *The Patriot*), doggedly attacked the superior British forces. The war was harsh for South Carolinians, pitting neighbor against neighbor, kin against kin. Plantations were looted and burned by both sides, but the most important conflicts, including the Battle of Cowpens, were solid patriot victories. Eventually, British General Charles Cornwallis was forced to abandon South Carolina, only to be cornered at Yorktown by General George Washington.

The Rise of King Cotton

After the Revolutionary War, there was a protracted recession, and the state came out of it facing the challenges of a new era. Low Country rice, once the foundation of South Carolina's wealth, was losing ground to rice grown on larger and more efficient rice plantations in Louisiana and Alabama. But as rice faded, the success of Sea Island cotton offered new hope to the economy. Sea Island cotton had long fibers and seeds that were fairly easy to remove by hand, making it viable for growers with a large slave labor force. True to its name, however, Sea Island cotton could only be grown along the coast. Inland, farmers were able to grow short-fiber Upland cotton, but its seeds were difficult to remove. The arrival of Eli Whitney's cotton gin changed all that, making a crop of unprecedented wealth possible in the Up Country and signaling South Carolina's second great wave of prosperity.

The post–Revolutionary War boom also brought a change in architectural styles. The ornate exteriors of the Georgian style—associated with European extravagance—gave way to the clean, unadorned façade's of the new Federal style, which reflected the conservative, egalitarian tones set by the country's founding fathers. However, the interiors of the Federal style homes became even more lavish. Championed by the English architects the Adam Brothers and early American architects including Thomas Jefferson, these houses featured sumptuous oval rooms, unsupported and majestically curved staircases, and even more ornate moldings, mantels, and cornices than their Georgian predecessors. One of the finest examples of Federal architecture is the Joseph Manigault House in Charleston, whose graceful open spaces are a testament to its architect.

Over the next few decades, settlers poured into South Carolina's Up Country, clearing land and planting cotton. Unlike rice, which could only be grown on land that could be flooded, cotton could be grown virtually anywhere across the seemingly endless, gently rolling land of South Carolina's Piedmont. By the mid-1800s, cotton was king throughout the state, and as more acres fell to cultivation, plantations got larger and even more prosperous, setting the stage for the final period of antebellum architecture: the great Greek Revival homes that are synonymous with the image of antebellum life.

The Greek Revival style began appearing in South Carolina as early as 1820 with homes such as the Rhett House in Beaufort. The name "Greek Revival" denotes the classical features taken from Greek and Roman architecture. In South Carolina, this style translated to grand, full-length (and later, wraparound), multistory porches with tall, tapering columns and ornate balustrades. Roofs were pitched lower and sported bold, triangular pediments at the gable ends and over porches. Many of these elegant features were meant primarily to impress the viewer, but the deep, column-supported porches also had a practical application: They shaded the large windows that were needed to let in breezes and provided a cool outdoor space for relaxing or entertaining.

Inside, many of these Greek Revival houses kept the functional two-over-two or four-over-four room plans that originated in the colonies' earlier Georgian homes. Instead of elaborate floor plans, the owners elected to display their wealth in ornate decoration: elegant carved panels, molded plaster medallions, marble mantles, ornate cornices, glittering chandeliers, European wallpapers, delicate wrought-iron balustrades, and paneled walls. A superb example of classic Greek Revival architecture is The Columns, completed in 1858, and named for the twenty-two magnificent Doric columns that support the plantation house's overarching hip roof.

Not all of the plantation houses built with the profits of cotton were built in the Greek Revival style, however. The amazing Kensington Mansion, built in 1852, is an extravagant and lavish example of Italian Renaissance architecture and was the personal vision of planter Matthew Richard Singleton.

Gardens also became increasingly important during this time. Small vegetable and flower gardens had been a part of plantation life for a hundred years, but the beginning of the eighteenth century saw a new idea: grand outdoor spaces filled with flowers, decorative shrubs, towering shade trees, inviting paths, cooling ponds, and fountains. These garden spaces functioned as an extension of the living space, existing purely for the enjoyment of the planter's family and guests. At the Hampton Preston Mansion in Columbia, Caroline Hampton created gardens that drew visitors from all over the United States and Europe. At Magnolia Plantation, the Reverend John Grimke Drayton, inspired by love, created gardens so spectacular that a Baedeker's travel guide of the period listed them along with the Grand Canyon and Niagara Falls as one the three most important attractions in America.

In the years leading up to the Civil War, the great wealth of South Carolina was held by fewer than a hundred families and was built largely by the sweat labor of tens of thousands of enslaved African Americans, whose life was anything but elegant. Knowing that the very existence of the great plantations depended on slave labor, and feeling overtaxed, threatened, and controlled by the more politically powerful Northern states, the leading politicians and affluent planters of South Carolina threw all of their wealth and political power into preserving their way of life.

South Carolina led the way to war, becoming the first state to secede from the Union. Many South Carolinians believed that if war came, it would be short and the Confederacy would be gloriously victorious. None could imagine the years of agony and bloodshed that would drain the South of her wealth and young men. Partly in punishment for the state's leadership role in the conflict, Union General William Tecumseh Sherman's troops burned scores of South Carolina's finest plantation homes in his infamous ride north. The flames and ashes marked an end to a way of life.

And that, perhaps, is the allure of the antebellum era. The drama of a world, which viewed through the mists of time, seems gracious, charming, and beautiful, yet is out of balance and doomed. It was a time that has passed into legend and cannot come again.

The plantation homes and historic houses that survived and are included here have been chosen for their architectural and historical significance, and because they are, at least on occasion, open to the public. They are among the far too few that have survived centuries of wars, earthquakes, fires, hurricanes, and the associated ravages of time. They stand as testaments to the vision of their builders and the loving care of those who have lived in them. These homes still stand today because their owners, preservationists, and other supportive organizations recognized their beauty and place in history and sought to preserve them for future generations.

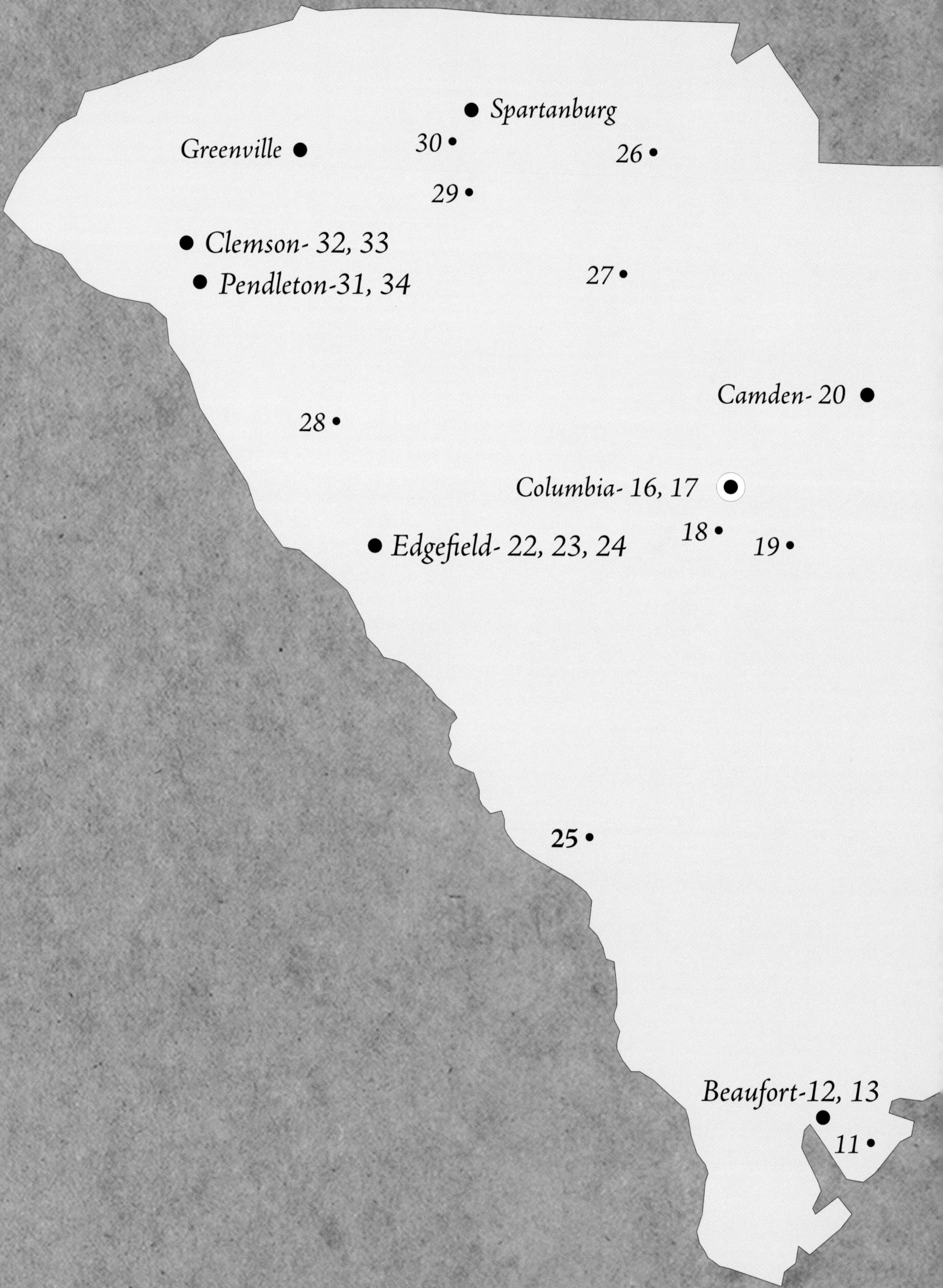

Spartanburg •

Greenville •

30 •

26 •

29 •

• Clemson- 32, 33

• Pendleton-31, 34

27 •

Camden- 20 •

28 •

Columbia- 16, 17 ◉

• Edgefield- 22, 23, 24

18 •

19 •

25 •

Beaufort-12, 13 •

11 •

HOUSES

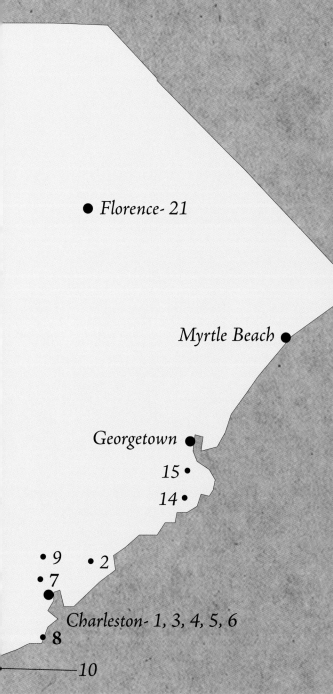

Florence- 21

Myrtle Beach

Georgetown

15

14

9   2

7

Charleston- 1, 3, 4, 5, 6

8

10

1. Aiken-Rhett House
2. Boone Hall Plantation
3. Edmondston-Alston House
4. Heyward-Washington House
5. Joseph Manigault House
6. Nathaniel Russell House
7. Drayton Hall
8. Magnolia Plantation
9. Middleton Place
10. The Grove
11. Frampton Plantation
12. John Mark Verdier House
13. The Rhett House
14. Hampton Plantation
15. Hopsewee Plantation
16. Hampton-Preston Mansion
17. Robert Mills House
18. Lorick Plantation House
19. Kensington Mansion
20. Kershaw-Cornwallis House
21. The Columns
22. Darby Plantation
23. Magnolia Dale
24. Oakley Park
25. Redcliffe Plantation
26. Brattonsville Homestead House
27. Rose Hill Plantation
28. Burt-Stark Mansion
29. Price House
30. Walnut Grove Plantation
31. Ashtabula Plantation
32. Fort Hill
33. Hanover House
34. Woodburn Plantation

Part I
LOW COUNTRY PLANTATIONS
& HISTORIC HOMES

CHARLESTON

Aiken-Rhett House

48 ELIZABETH STREET
CHARLESTON, SC 29401

Late in 1975, Francis Dill Rhett approached the Charleston Historic Society with an unusual offer: She wanted to know if the society would be interested in taking possession of her house to preserve it. What made the offer unusual was that Francis owned what had been one of Charleston's great antebellum homes, but for years, most of the house had been closed off and forgotten, while Francis lived in the few rooms with modern amenities. Imagine the sense of discovery that the society officials shared as they visited the house and pried open long-closed doors to gaze into vast rooms of faded glory, rooms that had, in the mid-1800s, hosted some of the grandest and most elegant parties Charleston had ever seen. As they moved from room to room, it became evident that amid the dust, faded wallpaper, and tattered furnishings lay part of the story of Charleston itself.

Solidly constructed of cypress and cedar, the Federal-style house was built in 1817 for Charleston merchant John Robinson. He was forced to sell it in 1825 after losing five ships at sea. The house was purchased by William Aiken Sr., who had made his fortune in rice, cotton, and railroads. In 1833, the house passed to his son, William Aiken Jr., who was elected governor of the state in 1844.

William Aiken Jr. and his wife, the lovely and dynamic Harriet Lowndes Aiken, made entertaining on a lavish scale the centerpiece of their public life. Shortly after taking possession of their new home, they began an extensive renovation, adding Greek Revival elements, restructuring the first floor, and adding the impressive curved twin marble staircase with cast-iron railings that greets visitors

today. They built a new three-story addition with dining room on the first floor, grand ballroom on the second, and bedchambers above. The couple also remodeled the two large drawing rooms on the first floor so they could be opened to form one grand space. These spaces, along with the large dining hall and wide porches (called "piazzas" in Charleston), could accommodate great numbers of guests. A family member reported that one party thrown by the Aikens in the mid-1850s was attended by more than five hundred guests.

FACING PAGE AND ABOVE:

AIKEN-RHETT HOUSE

Due to its distance from the waterfront, the house escaped major damage during the shelling of Charleston by Union forces during the Civil War, but it was looted a year later during the Union occupation of the town.

After the war and the death of Governor Aiken from pneumonia, his wife lived a reclusive life, using the grand ballroom as her bedroom until her death in 1892. At that time, the room was closed and not reopened until 1975. During the war, their daughter Henrietta married Confederate officer Andrew Burnett Rhett. Henrietta's sons (one of whom married Francis Dill) continued to live in the house, closing off more rooms over the years.

Rather than restore the house, the Historic Charleston Foundation chose to preserve the Aiken-Rhett House as it was, a near-perfect time capsule of antebellum life. Today, the once-ornate rooms are all but empty except for reminders here and there of the house's long-past glory—from the aging gilded mirrors, the ornate crystal chandeliers, and the faded furniture to the larger-than-life portrait of Harriet Lowndes Aiken, whose presence seems to be everywhere.

Boone Hall Plantation

1235 LONG POINT ROAD
MT. PLEASANT, SC 29464

As early as 1681, John Boone took possession of 430 acres along what was then called Wampacheone Creek. Boone primarily sold timber and other natural resources from the property, but the following four generations of Boones grew indigo as a cash crop, eventually expanding the plantation to more than 3,000 acres. The Boones sold the plantation in 1817.

After passing through numerous hands, it was purchased in 1843 by the industrious Horlbeck brothers, John and Henry. Sons of a successful Charleston builder and bricklayer, they had determined that the high-quality clay on the plantation was ideal for making bricks. They erected a brick factory and also purchased a cotton gin and began planting cotton. Operating these endeavors took manpower, and in a few years they increased Boone Hall's slave population from one hundred to five hundred.

Just before the Civil War, the Horlbecks decided to plant pecans on several hundred acres. This decision proved to be a prescient move, as the pecans were less labor-intensive than cotton and were in high demand after the war. Eventually, the Horlbecks expanded the plantation to more than 17,000 acres, including 15,000 pecan trees, making Boone Hall the largest and most productive pecan plantation in the country at the time.

Today, Boone Hall is still a working plantation, and some of its 738 remaining acres are under cultivation, growing strawberries, peaches, tomatoes, and other crops.

The current house is the fourth plantation dwelling at Boone Hall. The first house was swept away by a hurricane; the second house was destroyed by fire. The third house was deemed unsalvageable by the time the property was purchased by Thomas and Alexandra Stone in 1935. Their desire was to build a grand house reflecting regional architecture and history. They chose a Colonial Revival style that incorporated Federal and Greek Revival details. Most of the brick for the structure was already onsite—unsold leftovers from the Horlbeck brickyard. The Stones were so successful in creating the look and feel of a classic antebellum plantation that Hollywood has come calling more than once. In 1985, Boone Hall had a starring role as the set for the epic television miniseries *North and South*.

Among the most historically important features at Boone Hall are the outbuildings, including nine rare, brick slave quarters that make up one of the few remaining "slave streets" in the United States. There is also a well-preserved cotton gin and a round, brick smokehouse. The stunning live-oak allée creates a moss-draped tunnel of greenery through which approaching visitors glimpse the elegant façade of the main house. Experts are still debating the origins of the outbuildings, in particular the slave quarters, which some date to 1790, while others believe were added in the 1840s.

One of the high points of a visit to Boone Hall is a stroll through the five acres of gardens, whose graveled paths wind through thickets of azaleas, camellias, and beds of roses, some of which have been in cultivation since the 1600s. The grounds of Boone Hall are open daily, and there are regularly scheduled guided tours of the house.

FACING PAGE: BOONE HALL PLANTATION

FACING PAGE: BOONE HALL PLANTATION, SMOKEHOUSE

TOP: BOONE HALL PLANTATION, COTTON GIN

ABOVE: BOONE HALL PLANTATION, GARDEN

LEFT: BOONE HALL PLANTATION, SLAVE CABIN

Edmondston-Alston House

In 1817, the lean years of the post–Revolutionary War depression were over and Charleston was experiencing an economic boom. As the population increased, so did the need for housing, and the areas outside the old walled city began to be developed. At the extreme southern end of the city, the seawall was fortified, and the marshland behind it was filled in and divided into town lots. One of the first lot buyers was Charles Edmondston, a Charleston merchant who had amassed a fortune in shipping.

In 1825, Edmondston built an elegant Federal style house on the lot. The design was based on the Charleston "Single Houses" popular at the time, which made full use of the narrow, deep lots and maximized ventilation and light in all the rooms.

In the late 1820s and early 1830s, Edmondston suffered several reversals of fortune, culminating in the Panic of 1837 during which the price of a pound of cotton fell from 18 to 8 cents. Edmondston was forced to sell his house to satisfy creditors.

FACING PAGE, TOP:
EDMONDSTON-ALSTON HOUSE,
BATTERY STREET

FACING PAGE, BOTTOM:
EDMONDSTON-ALSTON HOUSE,
EXTERIOR DETAILS

The new purchaser was Charles Alston, son of William "King Billy" Alston, one of South Carolina's most successful planters. Charles Alston renovated the house in the Greek Revival style, adding the second-floor piazza, roof balustrade, and an ironwork balcony. He also added his family coat of arms to the front parapet.

In Alston's time, the first floor was used for business transactions and family dining. The second floor, with two large drawing rooms opening onto the expansive piazza, was for social activities and entertaining. The third floor contained the family's sleeping quarters. The outbuildings included a detached kitchen with servants' quarters above it and a carriage house with second-floor quarters for the coachman. In 1859, records show the Alstons had sixteen slaves living on the property.

On April 12, 1861, Confederate General P. T. Beauregard stood on the piazza of the house to watch the bombardment of Fort Sumter, the opening battle of the Civil War. Later that year, General Robert E. Lee took shelter there as fire swept through parts of the city.

For Charleston, the tide of the war changed in 1863 when Union forces laid siege to the city. For more than a year and a half, Union ships bombarded the waterfront and the city's south end. Mrs. Alston and her daughter Susan fled to a farm in Greenville, while Charles Alston remained to run their plantation near Georgetown. In spite of the house's prominent position on the battery, no record of serious damage exists.

The house was less fortunate during the severe hurricane of 1911, which left the first floor flooded for an extended period. The flooring was eventually repaired, and evidence of the new, higher floor can be seen in the low first step of the main stairs.

Today, the house is still owned by descendents of the Alstons and is open daily for tours. Almost all of the furnishings are original to the house or to the early Alstons. Of particular interest is the two-thousand-volume library, whose breadth of subjects reflects the Alstons' love of reading.

PREVIOUS PAGES: EDMONDSTON-ALSTON HOUSE

FACING PAGE, BOTTOM AND LEFT:
EDMONDSTON-ALSTON HOUSE, EXTERIOR
DETAILS

FACING PAGE, TOP: EDMONDSTON-ALSTON
HOUSE, PARLOR

ABOVE: EDMONDSTON-ALSTON HOUSE, LIBRARY

Heyward-Washington House

**87 CHURCH STREET
CHARLESTON, SC 29403**

The simple Georgian façade of this colonial townhouse conceals a handsome, ornate interior and elegant walled grounds. Built by Colonel Daniel Heyward in 1772, this house is the third to occupy this site, which appears as lot 72 in the 1694 Grand Model for the walled city of Charleston. Daniel built the house as a wedding present for his son Thomas Heyward Jr. and his new bride, Elizabeth Matthews Heyward.

At age twenty-six, Thomas Heyward Jr. was already a prominent lawyer. He had studied locally and in England; he was called to the English Bar in 1770 and to the Carolina Bar a year later. Dynamic and articulate, he was an ardent patriot. In February 1776, he traveled to Philadelphia as a member of the Second Continental Congress and became a signer of the Declaration of Independence. He was the commander of a company of the Charleston Artillery and was wounded in the Battle of Port Royal in 1779. After the occupation of Charleston by the British, Heyward was arrested along with twenty-eight other patriots and exiled to St. Augustine. He was released in 1781 and returned to Charleston where he remained a leading political figure until his death in 1809.

Later in life, Heyward spent more time at his Beaufort plantation and let his Charleston townhouse to his aunt, who utilized it as a boarding school for girls. In May 1791, the house was leased to George Washington during his stay in the city as part of his presidential tour. Washington is reported to have found the city "wealthy, gay and hospitable."

When the house was offered for sale in 1794, it was described as "twelve rooms, a fireplace in each, a cellar and a loft, a kitchen for cooking and washing with a cellar below and 5 rooms for servants above; a carriage house and stables; all of brick surrounded by brick walls." For the next 135 years, the house changed hands several times, serving as a boarding house, private residence, and bakery. In 1929, the Heyward-Washington House was purchased by the Charleston Museum and opened to the public.

FACING PAGE: HEYWARD-WASHINGTON HOUSE

Today's visitors will find the house much as it was described in 1794, or perhaps even better, as it contains one of the finest collections of eighteenth- and nineteenth-century American furniture ever gathered. Most of the furniture on display was produced in Charleston between 1740 and 1810, during which time more than 250 cabinetmakers plied their trade in the city. The Holmes bookcase in the withdrawing room is considered priceless and is a superb example of late-eighteenth-century American furniture. In the front parlor is another fine example of Charleston craftsmanship, a breakfast table built circa 1760. Also in this room are a matching settee, chair, and marble-top table, which are part of the original furnishings of Drayton Hall and date to 1740.

The walled grounds of the house include an original carriage house and detached kitchen. The formal gardens are both lovely and historically accurate, replicating the style of Charleston's colonial period.

THIS PAGE: HEYWARD-WASHINGTON HOUSE, GARDEN

FACING PAGE, TOP: HEYWARD-WASHINGTON HOUSE, PARLOR

FACING PAGE, BOTTOM: HEYWARD-WASHINGTON HOUSE, STUDY

Joseph Manigault House

350 MEETING STREET
CHARLESTON, SC 29403

In 1779, fifteen-year-old Joseph Manigault stood beside his grandfather, trembling but bravely resolute in his crisp new militia uniform. They were among Charleston's hastily gathered patriot forces, waiting orders to repel the massive British Army's pending attack on the city. Young Joseph had no way of knowing that he and his city would not only survive the conflict, but thrive, and that one day he would own one of the finest houses in Charleston.

Half a world away, his older brother, Gabriel, was in Geneva, Switzerland, gaining a classical education that would lead to a life-long love of architecture. Years later, Gabriel would use knowledge he gained from studying the works of architects Robert Adam and Charles Bulfinch to create for his younger brother the elegant and airy mansion that stands today at the corner of Meeting and John Streets.

This area was one of Charleston's first suburbs. After several years of post–Revolutionary War depression, Charleston was rapidly growing beyond its old walled boundaries. Joseph's uncle had set aside seventy-nine acres outside the original town to be subdivided into estates for the well-to-do merchant families. He died before his dream was realized, but Joseph inherited the choice corner lot and became one of the first to build on the land.

In 1803, the year building commenced on Joseph's house, new styles of architecture were becoming popular, and Gabriel was quick to integrate neoclassical ideas from Adam and Bulfinch into his design. Joseph's new house incorporated high ceilings and large, airy spaces that made it much more comfortable in the South Carolina summer. Grand windows let in light and coastal breezes, while curved lines and simple decoration gave an impression of clean, functional elegance that reflected the era's popular Republican ideals.

The home's graciousness is most evident in the curved staircase that rises in a single, sinuous arc to the second floor. It is one of the finest examples of curved staircases in Charleston. Above the stair's midpoint, a stunning Palladian window pours light into the entry hall. The lavish detail and spaciousness of the dining room suggest that the Manigaults enjoyed entertaining on a grand scale. The classical theme peaks here with double pilasters around the doors and windows and an ornate Greek urn-and-swag plaster design below the cornice.

FACING PAGE, TOP: JOSEPH MANIGAULT HOUSE

FACING PAGE, BOTTOM: JOSEPH MANIGAULT HOUSE, GATEHOUSE

Upstairs, the drawing room fills the entire west end of the second floor. Here too the ornate classical motif is reflected in the column-like pilasters around the windows and doors; the ornate cornice decorated with acanthus, scrolls, and grapevines; and the delicate mantle frieze featuring the goddess Demeter and the Cupids. Adam's architectural style depended on symmetry, and this room shows its importance; the north and south walls are virtually identical, and the fireplace and flanking doors are reflected by the three matching windows in the opposite wall.

Joseph Manigault continued to live in this house until his death in 1843 at the age of eighty. His son, Gabriel, sold the house in 1852, and it passed through several owners. Early attempts to preserve the house in the 1920s and 1930s had mixed success until it was purchased for the Charleston Museum, which renovated it and opened it to the public in 1949.

FACING PAGE, TOP: JOSEPH MANIGAULT HOUSE, PARLOR

FACING PAGE, BOTTOM: JOSEPH MANIGAULT HOUSE,
DINING ROOM

ABOVE: JOSEPH MANIGAULT HOUSE, STAIRCASE

TOP: NATHANIEL RUSSELL HOUSE

ABOVE: NATHANIEL RUSSELL HOUSE, GARDEN

FACING PAGE: NATHANIEL RUSSELL HOUSE

FOLLOWING PAGES: NATHANIEL RUSSELL HOUSE, DRAWING ROOM, DINING ROOM, AND STAIRCASE

Nathaniel Russell House

Perhaps no building reflects the wealth and charm of Charleston's golden age more than the Nathaniel Russell House. Nathaniel Russell arrived in Charleston as a young man in 1765. Although he began as an agent for mercantile interests based in his native Bristol, Rhode Island, he quickly set about amassing his own fortune as an independent merchant. At the age of fifty, he married socially connected Sarah Hopton. Sarah was thirty-six at the time and gave Russell two daughters. It is likely that Nathaniel and Sarah began planning a grand house when Russell bought the lot at 51 Meeting Street in 1790. The post–Revolutionary War depression, however, forced a delay, and it wasn't until 1803 that construction began.

The finished house that they moved into in 1808 was the talk of Charleston. It is a superb example of Federal-style architecture, which places an emphasis on open, airy spaces and the beauty of symmetry. The house's most dramatic feature is the elegant staircase that sweeps in a single unsupported spiral from the grand first-floor entry hall to the second and third floors. It is the finest example of a cantilevered or "freeflying" stairway surviving in Charleston.

Another striking feature is the four-sided bay that extends from the roof to the ground, creating space for architect Robert Adam–influenced elliptical rooms on each of the main floors. On the first floor, this room is the formal dining room. The first floor also contains a reception area that was once divided between a seating area for guests and clients and Russell's personal office. On the second floor, the magnificent staircase leads to the striking oval drawing room. With its warm salmon-colored walls, floor-length windows, ornate marble mantle, and intricately detailed cornices and plasterwork, it is both the most decorative and inviting room in the house. Throughout the house, doors and woodwork have been painstakingly painted with faux-woodgrain patterns that are authenticated reproductions of the original house decor.

Built of local Carolina gray brick, the house has withstood several disasters, including a tornado in 1811 that tore the roof off and the devastating earthquake of 1886 that caused extensive damage. During the Civil War, the house was owned by Governor R. F. W. Allston, who fled with his family during the eighteen-month-long bombardment of Charleston by Union forces. After the war, Mrs. Allston returned to find the house had been struck by three cannonballs, yet sustained little damage.

Finally, in 1989, Hurricane Hugo devastated much of the Low Country and significantly damaged the house. The hurricane had a silver lining for the Nathaniel Russell House, however, as it spurred an intensive restoration that has brought the home back to a condition similar to the days of Nathaniel and Sarah Russell.

Today, the Nathaniel Russell House is the flagship of the Historic Charleston Foundation, and every year thousands of visitors tour the house and gardens. The rooms are elegantly furnished with period antiques, many of which have histories tied to the house and families that have lived here.

ASHLEY RIVER

Drayton Hall

3380 ASHLEY RIVER ROAD
CHARLESTON, SC 29414

In 1738, George Washington was just six years old, the American Revolution was decades in the future, and Charleston was at the height of its golden era. From the city docks, a seemingly endless stream of ships carried rice to England, returning with gold and trade goods that made the city one of the richest ports in the world. Surrounding Charleston and stretching far inland lay the maze of river deltas dotted with plantations that produced this wealth. Some of the finest plantations lay along the banks of the Ashley River. Their homes nurtured some of America's wealthiest and most powerful families, but of all the great homes that stood here in the mid-eighteenth century only one remains today, Drayton Hall.

The fact that the house is still intact—having survived two major wars, a massive earthquake, and several hurricanes—is amazing enough. Even more surprising is that a visitor today will enter a house that is virtually unchanged since its creation more than two and a half centuries ago. Through ownership by seven generations of Draytons, the house has remained largely untouched by renovation, reconstruction, updating, or even the addition of modern conveniences. In some rooms, the blue paint on the walls is only the third coat of paint the walls have ever known.

John Drayton was the third generation of Draytons in the Charleston area. His grandfather had arrived from Barbados in 1670. His father owned many properties and lived on the adjoining Magnolia Plantation. By the 1730s, owning a plantation on the Ashley had become fashionable, and young, wealthy John Drayton knew the time was ripe for the creation of the grand home that would be referred to only half jokingly as "John Drayton's Palace." In 1738, Drayton answered an advertisement that stated:

> TO BE SOLD, a PLANTATION on Ashley River, 12 miles from Charles Town by water, formerly belonging to Jordan Roche, containing 350 acres, whereof 150 acres of it is not yet clear'd, with a very good Dwelling-house, kitchen and several out houses, with a very good orchard, consisting of all sorts of Fruit Trees.

Drayton bought the plantation and began work expanding it. His house took four years to build, creating a Georgian-Palladian masterpiece that may be the finest remaining example of this style in America.

Following the Palladian style, the living quarters are built above a raised basement that may have housed a warming kitchen, slave quarters, and other work spaces. Both the first and second

floors feature large rooms—a great hall on the first floor and ballroom on the second—that were used for entertainment on a grand scale. These are flanked by symmetrically arranged smaller rooms. Palladian elements are also visible in the unusual two-story, pediment-topped portico and in the ornate overmantel of the great room. The room design came from the 1727 pattern book of the famous English architect Inigo Jones.

The house as it stands today sits alone in a park-like setting of lawn and trees, but in the late 1700s, the house was surrounded by ornate formal gardens, particularly on the river side. Near the river stood a blacksmith shop and orangerie. On either side of the house were two-story flankers, one of which served as a kitchen, the other as a laundry and storehouse; the outline of their foundations can still be seen today. Other outbuildings—including a privy, barns, and slave quarters—completed the tableau of a busy, working country estate.

Life at Drayton Hall agreed with John Drayton, and he outlived three wives. At age fifty-nine, he took as his fourth wife Rebecca Perry, the seventeen-year-old daughter of an overseer; she bore him

TOP: DRAYTON HALL

ABOVE: DRAYTON HALL, GARDENS

three children in the remaining four years of his life. Drayton almost certainly grew rice and indigo and raised cattle at Drayton Hall in the colonial period, and his descendents extended the landholdings.

In 1865, Sherman's Union troops marched up the Ashley River road, setting fire to one great plantation after another, but Drayton Hall was spared. Family legend has it that young Dr. John Drayton, great-grandson of the first John Drayton, sent his family away and stayed to tend slaves who were either sick with smallpox or feigning the sickness on his orders. In any event, the Union troops heeded the quarantine flags he placed about the property and left Drayton Hall untouched.

In the years following the war, Dr. Drayton struggled financially and at one point even considered selling Drayton Hall for its bricks. He was saved from this drastic action by the discovery of phosphate deposits on the property, and like other plantation owners along the Ashley, he chose to allow strip mining of the land rather than lose it.

By the early twentieth century, the property was in the hands of Charlotta Drayton. The family had steadfastly refused to add electricity or plumbing to the house, and Charlotta, who had a house in Charleston, used the estate for "camp-outs" for a few weeks in spring and fall. After her death in 1969, her nephews sold Drayton Hall in 1974 to the National Trust for Historic Preservation, which operates it today.

The Trust chose not to restore the house, but to preserve and stabilize it. Today, visitors—including many students of architecture—come from all over the world to walk through the empty rooms of Drayton Hall and experience one of the most original and unchanged examples of Colonial-period architecture in the United States.

FACING PAGE, TOP: DRAYTON HALL, FIREPLACE

FACING PAGE, BOTTOM LEFT: DRAYTON HALL, GARDENS

FACING PAGE, BOTTOM RIGHT: DRAYTON HALL, PARLOR

ABOVE: DRAYTON HALL

Magnolia Plantation

Known internationally for its magnificent gardens, Magnolia Plantation is unique for many reasons, including the fact that it has been owned and operated by the same family, the Draytons, for more than 320 years.

The story of Magnolia Plantation begins around 1660, when Thomas Drayton and his son, Thomas Drayton Jr., left England for the New World. Their first stop was Barbados, but overcrowding, lawlessness, and hurricanes soon prompted Thomas Jr. to try his luck in the raw new colony of Carolina. Onboard the ship to Charleston, he met and fell in love with the lovely Anne Fox, daughter of wealthy Barbadian Stephen Fox. When they married, Ann's father offered a dowry that included the land along the Ashley River that would become Magnolia Plantation. Thomas Jr. and Ann built the first house on Magnolia in 1676, one hundred years before the American Revolution.

The first garden at Magnolia Plantation was planted by Anne and her mother, Phyllis. This small formal garden near the main house still exists. Successive generations of Draytons added to the gardens, and by the early 1700s, the gardens covered ten acres.

Throughout much of the eighteenth century, Magnolia was the epitome of a prosperous southern plantation. The Draytons expanded their lands to more than 1,100 acres, most of which was planted in highly lucrative rice and indigo.

A great-great-great-grandson of Thomas Drayton Jr., John Grimke Drayton, was studying for the ministry in the 1830s when his older brother was killed in a hunting accident, and he unexpectedly found himself in line to inherit Magnolia Plantation. His new wife, Julia Ewing Drayton of Philadelphia, was anxious about the limitations of plantation life. To help relieve her homesickness, John vowed turned Magnolia's gardens into a "Paradise on Earth." A gifted horticulturist, he was the first to bring azaleas into the country and among the first to plant camellias outdoors. He had studied the fine gardens of Europe and was an ardent follower of the movement toward blending gardens with nature.

FACING PAGE: MAGNOLIA PLANTATION

Today, John Grimke Drayton's "naturalist style" is still evident in the gardens at Magnolia. As visitors follow the winding paths away from the more formal gardens near the house, they will notice that the style of plantings becomes softer as the garden gradually merges with the natural beauty of the river and marshlands. Magnolia's fifty acres of gardens contain thousands of azaleas in hundreds of varieties and more than nine hundred varieties of camellias. There are also thousands of other plantings that create ever-changing patterns of color throughout the year.

Beyond the garden, a large riverfront tract has been set aside as a wetland nature reserve and has trails that lead along the old rice dikes. Inland, the Audubon Swamp Garden features boardwalks and trails that lead through the watery mysteries of a cypress swamp.

John Grimke Drayton's early life was influenced by his two aunts, both devout abolitionists. John became determined to give the slaves of Magnolia an education that went beyond basic religion. Defying state laws, he created a school at Magnolia that taught slaves the three R's. The school building is still standing today and used as an office.

During the Civil War, John's wife and children fled to Philadelphia. As the Union Army approached, John retreated to his country home in North Carolina. While there, he one day looked

out to see his foreman approaching. The man had walked 250 miles to tell John that the Union troops had burned the house at Magnolia. The soldiers left the gardens relatively untouched, however, and many of John's now-freed slaves had returned to tend them.

After the war, Drayton was forced to sell much of Magnolia's land to a mining company, who strip-mined it for phosphates. He retained the current 390 acres with its 50 acres of gardens; in 1870, he opened the gardens to the public.

Three years later, he was ready to reestablish Magnolia Plantation as his home. He purchased a solid Colonial-era cottage from a nearby plantation, disassembled it, and floated it ten miles upriver on barges to be erected on the site of the previous plantation homes at Magnolia.

The modest cottage was originally built in 1760, and Drayton set about updating and expanding it, adding several rooms to house his growing family. His additions included a porch with elegant tapered columns that gave the house a distinctly Greek Revival look. Drayton's daughter, Julie Drayton Hastie, made even more dramatic improvements around 1895, adding the large formal dining room, living room, and two bedrooms. She also added the stylish cupola on the roof, which contained a large water tank to supply running water throughout the house. Her additions, in particular the cupola, reflected the Victorian style of the day, yet they smoothly harmonized with the earlier neoclassical style created by her father.

Today, the house is the visual centerpiece of the estate and overlooks the magnificent gardens. A steady stream of visitors strolls the shady, flower-lined paths, just as they have for more than one hundred and thirty years, making the gardens the oldest manmade attraction in the United States.

FACING PAGE: MAGNOLIA PLANTATION

THIS PAGE: MAGNOLIA PLANTATION,
GARDENS

TOP: MAGNOLIA PLANTATION, AUDUBON SWAMP
GARDEN

FACING PAGE AND ABOVE: MAGNOLIA PLANTATION,
GARDENS

Middleton Place

4300 ASHLEY RIVER ROAD
CHARLESTON, SC 29414

To appreciate what has been lost at Middleton Place, you have only to stand in the middle of the estate's large, elliptical drive and look toward the river. The house that stands to your right seems imposing enough, until you realize that it was only a modest flanker to the original mansion. If you picture its twin to the left, then perhaps in between you can envision the grand, three-story, brick Jacobean-style mansion built in the early eighteenth century.

When Henry Middleton married Mary Williams in 1741, he was already one of the wealthiest men in America. He had a passion to create a country home that would reflect his status and rival the fine estates of England. Moreover, he wanted his grand house to be surrounded by fabulous formal gardens such as those becoming popular throughout Europe. Mary brought to Henry a dowry that gave him the ideal place to launch his dream—the gentle land along the Ashley River that would become Middleton Place.

THIS SPREAD: MIDDLETON PLACE

Middleton started his project on a grand scale, designing a magnificent house and laying out what was to become America's premier garden. Utilizing the style of André Lé Nôtre, designer of the gardens at Versailles, Middleton's rigorously formal design formed a perfect isosceles triangle covering more than sixty-five acres. The gardens, which required extensive reshaping of the land as well as planting and tending countless trees, shrubs, and flowerbeds, took a workforce of more than one hundred slaves ten years to complete.

Visitors today find the gardens little changed since Middleton's time. The central feature is the broad lawn that leads from the main house site to the river. Gentle, step-like terraces descend to two large ponds shaped like the open wings of a butterfly. The center of the design is taken up by a series of room-like gardens: an octagon where gentlemen once played at bowls and a wheel-shaped sundial garden filled with roses. Here and there are quiet sanctuaries, sheltered by boxwoods; benches offer respite and places

from which to contemplate the surrounding flowers and statuary. One side of the garden is bounded by a long reflecting pool, where swans and ducks paddle.

While the Middletons' garden survived wars and natural disasters, the main house was less fortunate. During the Civil War, the house was owned by Henry Middleton's great grandson, Williams Middleton, who was a staunch supporter of the Confederacy. In 1865, Union troops looted the elegant mansion and set it afire. Its flame-scorched ruins stood until the earthquake of 1893 leveled them.

In the dark years after the war, Williams held on to Middleton Place by selling the phosphate rights to a mining company. He restored the partially damaged south flanker as his home and furnished it with items he had hidden from the Union Army.

In the 1920s, Middleton descendent John Pringle Smith inherited the property and began restoring the gardens to their former grandeur. In the 1930s, he opened the gardens to the public, and in 1975 he opened the house for tours under the direction of the newly created Middleton Place Foundation.

ABOVE AND FACING PAGE:
MIDDLETON PLACE: RICE MILL
AND POND

LEFT: MIDDLETON PLACE,
GARDEN

EDISTO ✤ ISLAND

The Grove

One of the most visually charming plantations in the Low Country, The Grove is an elegant Greek Revival home fronted by deep, inviting two-story porches supported by graceful columns. The Grove's signature features, however, are the unusual polygonal rooms on either side of the main floor; the rooms feature elegant bays that offer sweeping views of the plantation lands.

Situated at the juncture of the Edisto and Dawho rivers, The Grove was originally part of a land grant made in 1694 to Robert Fenwick, who had served as one of the Red Sea Men—privateers who preyed on non-Christian ships in the Indian Ocean.

After trading hands several times, the land was purchased in 1825 by George Washington Morris, son of Revolutionary War hero Colonel Lewis Morris. George Morris built The Grove in 1828, and lived there with his wife Maria. In 1834, however, George succumbed to malaria. Maria was left to manage an estate that included several plantations totaling 4,588 acres and having more than one hundred slaves. Her family tried to convince her to sell her land, but with steely resolve, Maria refused. Under her, the plantation flourished, producing bountiful rice crops, and she used her first profits to purchase a schooner to

THIS SPREAD: THE GROVE

transport freight for her neighbors. Within three years, she paid off her husband's debts and had enough money left over to have the house plastered.

Unfortunately, Maria's son, George Morris Jr., who took over operations in 1855, lacked his mother's business acumen. Legend has it that one of his greater accomplishments was to teach his horse to carry him up the outside staircase of the house and deposit him at the top when he was too drunk to walk. In 1857, deeply in debt and in poor health, George was found hanging from a tree, an apparent suicide.

Maria then sold The Grove to John Berkley Grimball, owner of a neighboring plantation. Grimball and his wife Meta moved into The Grove and were delighted with life there. Meta's journal writings tell of pleasant evenings spent in the parlor, playing music, reading, sewing, and talking, but their contentment was not long lived.

The Civil War brought hard times, and the Grimballs were forced to flee. The Grove was looted and fell into disrepair. At the end of the war, Grimball regained his property only after signing an oath of allegiance to the federal government. But with no funds for rebuilding, he was forced to sell The Grove to pay his debts.

The years passed, and The Grove was passed from owner to owner. The first refurbishment came in the 1930s when Owen Winston of Brooks Brothers purchased the estate for a hunting retreat. In 1992, the house passed to the U.S. Fish and Wildlife Service, who performed archeological excavations and substantially renovated and restored the house.

Today, The Grove is the headquarters for the Ernest F. Hollings ACE Basin National Wildlife Refuge and is surrounded by the unique, 6,300-acre wetland ecosystem that lies between the Edisto and Dawho rivers. The Grove's once-productive rice fields are now flooded to make habitat for a dazzling array of waterfowl and other birds. The property is open to the public daily, and there is a small interpretive center in the house.

BEAUFORT

Frampton Plantation

1 LOWCOUNTRY LANE
YENASSE, SC 29945

When John Frampton became a signer of South Carolina's Declaration of Succession in 1860, his family had lived on their plantation lands for over a century. The land was originally part of a king's grant from the early 1700s that included thousands of acres in Beaufort and Jasper counties and was divided among the Frampton family members. The region became know as The Hill, as it occupies the highest ground for miles around.

Little is known of the original dwelling that John Frampton and his family lived in prior to the Civil War. What is known is that he raised cotton and rice on an extensive landholding with the help of more than 130 slaves.

As Sherman's army approached in 1865, Frampton fled with his family. Nearby Beaufort was occupied through much of the war by the Union Army, who used the town's elegant homes as hospitals and administration centers and so saved most of the buildings from destruction. Frampton's home, however, was too far from Beaufort to be spared, and with his bold signature on the Declaration of Secession, the fate of his home was sealed. Sherman's troops burned Frampton's house and outbuildings to the ground.

Yet unlike many of his contemporaries, Frampton still held substantial assets after the war, and by 1868 he had returned to his plantation lands and built a new home.

Frampton's second home is unusual in that it presents a charming blend of traditional Greek Revival features along with some early Victorian elements, which began appearing in South Carolina after the Civil War. The house originally featured a classical two-level porch, the upper level of which was accessed by French doors from the second-floor hallway. The traditional four-over-four room design was modified by elongating rooms on one side, creating an L-shaped façade that increases ventilation through the house. Other interesting elements include the elegant three-sided bay windows, which add welcome light to the front parlor, and an inviting entry door flanked by sidelights. Beyond the front door, the entry hall leads to an ornate staircase that rises gracefully to the second floor. There are a total of seven fireplaces throughout the house, and the floors are heart-of-pine.

THIS SPREAD: FRAMPTON PLANTATION AND DETAIL

Indoor plumbing, wiring, and a kitchen were added to the house about 1930. In the 1970s it served as a sales office for Sea Pines Realty, which was undertaking the development of nearby Hilton Head Island.

In 1993, the building was purchased by the Lowcountry & Resort Islands Tourism Commission and extensively renovated for use as a visitors center. Today, the two front parlors of the house serve as a gift shop and museum. Directly behind the house, visitors can see earthworks erected by General Lee's Confederate troops to shield the guns that defended the nearby Charleston and Savannah Railway.

Both the front and the back of the house are shaded by massive live oaks draped with Spanish moss. The trees are between 250 and 300 years old, and they probably look much as they did when John Frampton sat on the porch to drink sweet tea so many years ago.

John Mark Verdier House

801 BAY STREET
BEAUFORT, SC 29902

In the mid-1790s, as John Mark Verdier chafed impatiently in a Charleston debtors prison, he may well have used the time to begin planning what would become one of Beaufort's finest Bay Street houses. Designing an elegant home while imprisoned for unpaid debts might seem bold, but Verdier was both an optimist and a risk-taker. A descendent of Franco-Swiss Huguenots who arrived in the Carolina Colony from the West Indies, Verdier had grown wealthy as a merchant in Beaufort, specializing in the export of rice and indigo. The post–Revolutionary War depression, however, along with five years of poor crops, had brought him to the edge of ruin.

Historians have examined the architectural detail of Verdier's house and determined that it was most likely constructed between 1801 and 1805. By that time, Verdier had reestablished his mercantile business. He had also acquired large landholdings on Lady's and Hilton Head Islands, on which he began to grow a new crop that was well-suited to the climate and also highly profitable—Sea Island cotton.

The Verdier House is a simple, elegant Federal-style home designed to fit on the narrow town lot at the corner of Bay and Scott's Streets. The exterior shows the clear influence of architect Robert Adam in the two-tiered, pediment-topped portico sheltering the front entrance, as well as in the balanced placement of the windows and the Palladian fanlight over the front door. The unusual entry, modified in the 1870s, consists of two sets of steps beginning from opposite directions along the sidewalk and rising above an arched landing to the center of the first-level portico. Local legend says the Marquis de Lafayette addressed the citizens of Beaufort from this portico during his tour of America in 1825. Although no written account of this event has been found, for much of the twentieth century the house was locally referred to as the Lafayette House.

Inside, several interesting features depart from the classic four-over-four design so popular at the time. The entry hall starts at the front door, passes through an ornately columned arch, and widens to accommodate a graceful central stairway. The stairway rises to a landing below an eye-catching Palladian window; above the first landing, the staircase splits into flights that rise left and right to the second floor.

The large first-floor parlor was probably used frequently for entertaining and features full-length wall paneling, dentilated cornices, and an ornate mantle with a marble surround. Upstairs, the front room extends two-thirds of the width of the house, creating a grand ballroom. A smaller adjacent room is accessed via a pair of doors, suggesting that it was opened to the ballroom during festivities.

During the Civil War, Beaufort fell to the Union Army, and the Verdier House was used as a headquarters. After the war, Verdier's daughter-in-law was forced to pay $150 to regain ownership of the house, and it remained in the Verdier family until the 1940s. By then, the house was in such poor condition that there was talk of razing it. Fortunately, preservation-minded citizens interceded and the house was saved.

In 1968 the house was acquired by the Historic Beaufort Foundation, which fully restored it and opened it to the public in 1976.

FACING PAGE, TOP: JOHN MARK VERDIER HOUSE

FACING PAGE, BOTTOM: JOHN MARK VERDIER HOUSE, PARLOR

ABOVE: JOHN MARK VERDIER HOUSE, BEDROOM

The Rhett House

1009 CRAVEN STREET
BEAUFORT, SC 29902

In 1820, Thomas Smith and his wife Caroline Barnwell decided to build a summer townhouse as a retreat from the stifling heat of their working plantation on the Ashepoo River. They chose a lot not far from the waterfront in the burgeoning port of Beaufort, where summer sea breezes sweep up the Broad River, keeping the air cooler and relatively free of mosquitoes.

The house that Thomas and Caroline built has large windows and open rooms to take advantage of those summer breezes. While the front parlors are of a traditional size and design, the back rooms were narrower to facilitate airflow through the house and to leave room on the narrow lot for a garden and outbuildings. They were quick to incorporate the new Greek Revival style, creating full-length Charleston-style piazzas supported by fourteen stylish Corinthian columns. The piazzas

not only offered the family a place to enjoy outdoor living through the summer months, but they also shaded the south-facing front windows from the summer sun, leaving the parlors cooler in midday.

The Rhett house was not large by Charleston standards, but it incorporated delicate and ornate details that tastefully announced the affluence of the owners. One of the most impressive features of the house is the decorative panel, carved in a delicate, twin-palm-frond pattern and supported by carved pilasters, that spans the lower hallway, defining the entry space. Beyond the carved panel, the stairs rise in two flights lit by a large Palladian window. The fireplace mantles in both parlors feature ornate plaster-work decorated with garlands, Greek figures, and seashells. Also of note is the doorway that leads to the second-floor piazza. Flanked by sidelights and topped with a Palladian fanlight and decorative lintels, it is yet another indication that the Rhetts were well-to-do.

THIS SPREAD: THE RHETT HOUSE

The Rhett name made a rather sudden appearance in Beaufort history. In 1837, Thomas Smith was one of eighteen Smith family members who changed their name to Rhett to share in the inheritance of a wealthy relative, who was childless and did not want to see his ancestral name disappear.

Just prior to the Civil War, the large piazzas were extended around the west side of the house, and the number of columns increased to twenty. During the Civil War, Beaufort fell to the Union Army, who used the town as a hospital and administrative center. Photographs from the period show that the Rhett House was used to nurse wounded and sick soldiers.

Today, the house is operated as a fine inn and has hosted stars such as Barbara Streisand, Sandra Bullock, Gwyneth Paltrow, and Dennis Quaid. The current owners have made tasteful additions to the rear of the house and finished the basement to create additional guest rooms. In the west parlor, which is now a dining room, hang several historic photos that show the progressive changes to this historic house.

GEORGETOWN AREA & THE SANTEE RIVER

Hampton Plantation

1950 RUTLEDGE ROAD
McCLELLANVILLE, SC 29458

When Daniel Horry Jr. inherited Hampton Plantation after his father's death in 1763, his inheritance included the original six-room farmhouse. It had been built sometime between 1730 and 1750 by his French Huguenot ancestors, who had fled persecution in Europe and arrived in South Carolina in the 1690s. Daniel's second wife was Harriott Pinckney, whose mother, Eliza Pinckney, had gained fame for developing the process to turn indigo into dye. By family accounts, Harriet was every bit as intelligent and industrious as her mother. Together she and Daniel expanded their plantations on Wambaw Creek to more than five thousand acres, on which they successfully produced rice and indigo.

Early in their marriage, Daniel and Harriet decided to renovate and expand their house—and expand it they did! They added two large rooms to fill out the second story. Then they designed and built the two grand, two-story wings that flank the house. The East Wing contains a single ballroom, whose gracefully curved cove ceiling is painted traditional sky blue and soars to a height of twenty-six feet. The floor of the ballroom is laid with unbroken thirty-foot lengths of pine; on one wall, a massive fireplace was once lined with painted tiles. The West Wing incorporates a large, ornate dining room that spans the wing and takes up half its depth. The dining room, too, has a lofty ceiling, and as a result, two false windows were added to the outside front façade of the house to maintain its elegant Georgian symmetry.

If family legends are true, the portico at the Hampton Plantation house may be the first design in the area to be inspired by architect Robert Adam. The Pinckney family had spent years in England and were great fans of the famous stage actor, Garrick. Eliza and Harriott greatly admired Garrick's fashionable house in Hampton Gardens. It is likely that they named Hampton Plantation after it, as well as borrowing the design of its stylish two-story front portico for the newly renovated plantation house.

The house's impressive portico was completed in 1791, just in time for a breakfast visit by George Washington, who passed through the area on his presidential tour. It is said that Washington admired

the large oak that stands in front of the portico and urged the Horrys to preserve it. Today, the ancient "Washington oak" still stands.

The house's last live-in owner was South Carolina's beloved poet laureate, Archibald Rutledge. Descended from a long line of Rutledges that married into the Horry family, Archibald spent his joyous boyhood at Hampton; and he returned to live here after his retirement in 1937. A widely acclaimed naturalist and writer, he extensively restored the old homestead, recording that labor of love in his 1941 book *Home by the River*. Rutledge left Hampton Plantation to the South Carolina State Park Service, and today the plantation house is open to the public for daily tours.

THIS SPREAD: HAMPTON PLANTATION

The house is preserved as a museum of eighteenth- and nineteenth-century American building styles. The rooms are unfurnished, and in places plaster and lath have been removed to create "windows" that reveal the house's inner construction styles, which span almost two centuries.

Hopsewee Plantation

494 HOPSEWEE ROAD
GEORGETOWN, SC 29440

Built between 1735 and 1740 by Thomas Lynch Sr., Hopsewee Plantation is South Carolina's only remaining birthplace of a signer of the Declaration of Independence. Lynch Sr.'s father, Thomas Lynch I, had developed several plantations along the Santee River. Lynch Sr. purchased the land that eventually became Hopsewee around 1730.

Thomas Lynch Sr. built his sturdy post-and-beam home out of black cypress, which is known for resisting the destructive humidity of the Low Country. The house is a classic four-over-four design set atop a brick basement. The elegance of the Hopsewee home is understated; there are hand-carved moldings and cornices in the main rooms and heart-of-pine floors throughout. The house features full-length porches that overlook the Santee River, whose waters in the mid-eighteenth century bustled with constant boat traffic traveling between Charleston and the busy river plantations.

The Hopsewee house's simple, sturdy substance suited the Lynch family. Lynch Sr. was a highly respected figure in the community and a passionate patriot. He served as a representative of South

Carolina in the First Continental Congress. One of his fellow Congress attendees described Lynch, saying, "He wears the manufacture of this country, is plain, sensible and above ceremony, and carries with him more force in his very appearance than most powdered folk do in their conversation."

In 1775, Lynch, along with Benjamin Franklin and Colonel Benjamin Harrison, served as an advisor to General George Washington. In 1776, he returned to Philadelphia as a representative to the Second Continental Congress, but suffered a stroke and could not continue. His son, Thomas Lynch Jr., who was born and raised at Hopsewee, was unanimously elected to his father's position by the South Carolina Second Provincial Congress. He arrived at Philadelphia in time to become a noted participant, and at age twenty-six, he was the fifty-second signer of the Declaration of Independence.

Unfortunately, neither father nor son fared well after that. Lynch Sr. died on the journey home and was buried in Annapolis, Maryland. Lynch Jr. suffered from a fever—probably malaria. In order to improve his health, he and his wife, Elizabeth Shubrick Lynch, sailed for France via the West Indies in 1779, but their ship was lost at sea.

Before his death, Thomas Lynch Sr. sold Hopsewee to Robert Hume in 1762, and the house remained in the Hume family for almost two centuries. In 1972, Hopsewee was designated a National Historic Landmark. Frank and Raejean Beattie took over the Hopsewee plantation house in 2001, opening it to the public and offering "attic-to-cellar tours."

The house is furnished with eighteenth- and nineteenth-century furniture pieces, many of which came from the Beatties' personal collection. The Beatties have helped arrange archaeological excavations of several ancient slave cabins on the property and display collections of pottery, buttons, coins, and jewelry that have been found on the grounds.

Frank Beattie sometimes reminisces about growing up in the area and rowing along the Santee as a boy with family friend, Archibald Rutledge, South Carolina's poet laureate who lived at nearby Hampton Plantation. "We would row past Hopsewee, and he would tell me about how important its history was," Beattie recollects, "but I never thought I would own it."

THIS SPREAD: HOPSEWEE PLANTATION, SLAVE CABIN

Part II
UP COUNTRY PLANTATIONS
& HISTORIC HOMES

Hampton-Preston Mansion

1615 BLANDING STREET
COLUMBIA, SC 29201

Originally built in 1818 by successful merchant Ainsley Hall, this house is better known for its flamboyant second owner, Wade Hampton I. According to family tradition, Hampton came to Columbia in 1823 looking for a townhouse where he and his third wife, Mary Cantey Hampton, could escape the swampy conditions and isolation of their Congaree River Plantation. He so admired Hall's new home—a stately four-over-four Federal-style brick mansion with a slate hip roof—that he offered to purchase it. Hall refused. Undaunted, Hampton made two more offers. The last, at the princely sum of $35,000, was too good for Hall to turn down.

The Hamptons made modest changes to the house's decor. They added a pediment-topped roofline and stuccoed the exterior of the house to create a cut-stone look.

If their changes to the house were minor, Mary's transformation of the grounds was nothing short of astounding. In a project that continued throughout her life, Mary began turning the four acres around the house into one of the most elaborate and celebrated gardens in the South. Descriptions of her gardens appeared in numerous publications, and eventually the gardens gained such renown that they were visited by many luminaries, including the famous naturalist James Audubon.

At the time of his death in 1835, Wade Hampton was believed to be the wealthiest man in the Carolinas—and possibly in the country. Between 1848 and 1850, his daughter Caroline and

FACING PAGE: HAMPTON-PRESTON MANSION

BELOW: HAMPTON-PRESTON MANSION, DETAILS

son-in-law John Preston undertook major renovations of the house, building a rear addition that doubled its size. The main entrance was relocated so it faced Mary's beautiful gardens. They also created the Greek Revival–style portico on the Blanding Street side and built two large flankers that contained a kitchen, slave quarters, and John's law offices.

The family lived in the house through much of the Civil War, but eventually fled to York County when the Union Army occupied Columbia and used the house as a headquarters. It was one of the few homes in Columbia not burned during Sherman's march, reportedly because a group of Ursuline nuns requested that it be spared for their quarters.

After the war, the Prestons were forced to sell their home. It briefly served as the governor's mansion, and from 1890 to 1930, it housed two different women's colleges—the College for Women and Chicora College. After the colleges moved on, the property was subdivided and declined into a gritty urban maze of apartment complexes and light industrial buildings.

The rebirth of the Hampton-Preston Mansion began in 1968, when the State of South Carolina purchased the property. The commercial buildings were torn down, the large addition built by the Prestons was removed, and the house was restored to its pre-1850s appearance. Today, the Historic Columbia Foundation operates the house as a museum open to the public for tours. Each room of the house is decorated to represent a different period of its nineteenth-century history. There are even plans to begin restoring the famous gardens that once were the pride of Columbia.

FACING PAGE, TOP: HAMPTON-PRESTON MANSION, PARLOR

FACING PAGE, BOTTOM: HAMPTON-PRESTON MANSION, DINING ROOM

ABOVE: HAMPTON-PRESTON MANSION, REAR FACADE

Robert Mills House

In 1823, when wealthy Wade Hampton I offered Columbia merchant Ainsley Hall the incredible sum of $35,000 for his house (see the Hampton-Preston Mansion), Hall accepted. Unfortunately, Hall hadn't consulted his wife about the transaction. To allay her anger at selling their nearly new home, he purchased the lot across the street and began planning an even more sumptuous residence.

Unfortunately, Hall suddenly fell ill and died shortly after construction began. His wife, contending with legal issues over the estate, was forced to sell the building shortly after its completion, so it was never used as a private residence.

Today, the house is not named for Hall, but for the architect he hired to design it, Robert Mills. Born in Charleston in 1781, Mills developed an early passion for designing buildings and went on to become the first American-born and American-trained architect. His education came under the tutelage of James Hoban, who designed the U.S. White House; Thomas Jefferson, who took Mills into his family and trained him in classical construction styles; and Benjamin Latrobe, principal designer of the U.S. Capitol, who gave Mills an understanding of the science and engineering of great buildings. During his career, Mills designed edifices throughout South Carolina, but is best known for his public buildings in Philadelphia, Baltimore, and Washington, D.C. Among his most famous designs are the Old Post Office, the U.S. Treasury, and the Washington Monument.

INSET: ROBERT MILLS HOUSE, DEPENDENCY

FACING PAGE, TOP: ROBERT MILLS HOUSE

FACING PAGE, BOTTOM: ROBERT MILLS HOUSE, PARLOR

The house that Mills designed for Hall blends elements from several popular styles of the era. The basic structure reflects the neoclassical style. The front façade has much in common with the imposing public structures Mills designed, incorporating a classical, Jeffersonian two-story portico supported by four grand Ionic columns. There are also some elegant Palladian features, such as the front door with its sidelights and fanlight, Venetian windows, and an apse niche that shelters a side door. The rear façade is remarkably different and much more intimate in style than the front of the house, sporting an ornately arcaded, almost Italianate-style piazza that spans the width of the building.

Inside, the first floor has a classic four-room design. Two parlors open into a broad central hallway. There is also a formal dining room and somewhat smaller library. A second dining room in the basement was intended for the family to use when not entertaining. On the second floor, Mills diverges from the four-room plan to allow for two large dressing rooms off the two largest bedrooms, a popular option in the early nineteenth century.

The Presbyterian Synod of South Carolina purchased the Halls' house in 1830 for use as a theological seminary. Two large flankers were built on either side as dormitories, and the property remained a school for more than one hundred years.

In 1963, the house was slated for demolition, but was purchased by the Historic Columbia Foundation. The group undertook a four-year renovation of the home and grounds, then opened it to the public. Inside, the house is decorated with a superb collection of Federal, Regency, and Empire furnishings.

PAGE 74: ROBERT MILLS HOUSE, BATHROOM

PAGE 75, TOP: ROBERT MILLS HOUSE, PARLOR

PAGE 75, BOTTOM: ROBERT MILLS HOUSE, DINING ROOM

RIGHT: ROBERT MILLS HOUSE, GARDENS

BELOW: ROBERT MILLS HOUSE, KITCHEN

ABOVE: ROBERT MILLS HOUSE

LEFT: ROBERT MILLS HOUSE, FRONT DOORWAY

Lorick Plantation House

2184 NORTH LAKE DRIVE
(OLD BUSH RIVER ROAD)
IRMO, SC 29063

In the mid-1800s, Up Country plantation houses were built for comfort and functionality, and the house that George Lorick erected in 1840 on his Irmo plantation was no exception. Cotton was the dominant crop throughout the Up Country, and the 1850 census showed that Lorick owned 7,650 acres—more than twelve square miles of land—much of which was cleared and under cultivation.

Like many Up Country plantation owners, Lorick was a descendant of hard-working Scot immigrants, who tended to avoid blatant displays of opulence and grandeur. In spite of this, Lorick found subtle ways to display his growing wealth in his new home. His affluence is quietly reflected in the ten-foot-high ceilings, hand-pegged floors, crystal chandeliers, and the fine wainscoting that decorates the foyer, parlor, and dining room.

His finished house was a classic Up Country plantation. It had two full stories and a deep, hip-roofed porch that spanned the front façade, supported by stately pillars. Upstairs, the house featured two bedrooms that opened onto a wide central hall. The hall led to the house's dominant feature, a Greek Revival–style second-floor balcony located above the porch and shaded by a classic pediment roof supported by pillars. The first floor featured a grand formal dining room and spacious parlor; the kitchen was located behind the house in a separate building. Over the years, additions were made, eventually expanding the house to include eleven rooms.

FACING PAGE, TOP: LORICK PLANTATION HOUSE

FACING PAGE, BOTTOM: LORICK PLANTATION HOUSE

Toward the end of the Civil War, detachments of Sherman's troops conducted raids throughout the area and plundered several local plantations. Union officers camped in Lorick's house, reputedly keeping cattle on the first floor, butchering them, and cooking the meat in the fireplaces. Legend has it that as the Union troops left the pillaged house, they scattered live coals from the fireplaces across the floors and rode off. The house began to burn. Fortunately, the Lorick family returned in time to put out the fire before extensive damage occurred.

The house remained in the Lorick family until 1937. As various owners sold land from the original plantation, the town of Irmo began growing around the house. In 1943, Harold Lorick, a descendent of George Lorick, bought the house. Harold built a racetrack on the property, and for many years, the regular carriage races that took place there provided excitement and made Lorick's a social gathering place for the community.

In 1995, the house was moved twelve miles to its present location. Unlike many house-moving operations, which involve cutting the house into sections, the Lorick House was moved in a single piece, which included all eleven rooms and measured thirty-four feet wide by thirty-five feet high. Power lines were dropped and traffic diverted during the seven-hour move. At its new location, the interior of the house was extensively renovated to be the Lake Murray Country visitor center. Care was taken to keep the original exterior appearance, and today, the outside of the house looks much as it did when it was built more than one hundred and sixty years ago.

Kensington Mansion

When Matthew Richard Singleton returned from an extensive tour of Europe in the early 1840s, he was already a wealthy man. His plantation, then known as Head Quarters, encompassed more than 6,600 acres, including almost 3,000 acres in crops. Surrounding his house, vast fields of cotton, rice, sweet potatoes, wheat, and rye spread to the horizon. In 1844, Singleton married Martha Rutledge Kinloch and renamed his estate Kensington, in honor of her childhood home.

It was a prosperous time for plantation owners in South Carolina, and many were renovating their homes in the new Greek Revival style. Singleton longed to create a magnificent house at Kensington, but he wanted something different. He dreamed of building a home incorporating the graceful architecture he had seen in the villas of Italy and southern France.

In 1852, Charleston architect Francis Lee traveled to Kensington and laid out the foundation for an extravagant Italianate mansion that would be built around and incorporate Singleton's existing Georgian-style house. With the addition of two large wings, the new house featured twenty-nine rooms and twelve thousand square feet of living space. Amazingly, the house took just two years to complete—a comparatively short building time considering the size and complexity of the project. Much of the work was accomplished by the skilled craftsmen among Singleton's 235 slaves.

FACING PAGE, TOP:
KENSINGTON MANSION

FACING PAGE, BOTTOM:
KENSINGTON MANSION,
GENTLEMEN'S PARLOR

INSET: KENSINGTON
MANSION

Unfortunately, Matthew Singleton never got to enjoy his new home. As work crews completed the interior painting, Singleton succumbed to illness and died in 1854. The house remained in the family until 1910, but then passed through numerous hands, eventually falling into disrepair. At one point, it was used as a barn for storing hay.

In 1981, the Kensington plantation house was acquired by International Paper, which began an extensive renovation to bring the house back to its former grandeur. The house is operated by a nonprofit foundation and is open to the public for tours, weddings, and other functions.

Today, Kensington looks much as it did in Singleton's time. Visitors enter the house to stand in the magnificent two-story entrance hall; the ceiling of that hall rises more than sixty feet to a domed roof topped with skylights that fill the space with light. The entry hall is encircled at the second-floor level by a balcony, whose delicate wrought-iron railings feature an intricate pattern of honeysuckle blossoms and leaves. A passage leading from the entry hall to the dining room is lined with niches for statuary and other *objets d'art*. The stunning dining room has an ornately gilded barrel-vaulted ceiling and a dramatic bank of windows that looks out toward the river. Throughout the downstairs rooms, the decorative plasterwork, particularly the cornices in the entry hall and parlors, is elaborate and of the highest quality.

The house's outside architecture is dominated by heavily arcaded porches, whose massive arched columns give it a sense of graceful solidity. The house is surrounded by an expansive lawn shaded by many trees, including some ancient, massive live oaks that may have sheltered Matthew Singleton as he watched his dream house being built.

PAGE 82: KENSINGTON MANSION, ENTRANCE HALL

PAGE 83: KENSINGTON MANSION, DINING ROOM

TOP: KENSINGTON MANSION, BEDROOM

ABOVE: KENSINGTON MANSION, DETAILS

FACING PAGE, TOP: KENSINGTON MANSION, GARDENS

FACING PAGE, BOTTOM: KENSINGTON MANSION, LADIES' PARLOR

Kershaw-Cornwallis House

222 BROAD STREET
CAMDEN, SC 29020

Few houses in antebellum South Carolina have seen as much history as Camden's Kershaw-Cornwallis House, and fewer still have burned to the ground, only to rise again from the ashes.

Built in 1777 by Joseph Kershaw, this classic Georgian home was patterned on Charleston's finest homes of the period. Kershaw was a successful merchant who arrived in Camden in 1758, when it was a raw frontier outpost. Seeing opportunities for growth, Kershaw bought land and started several mills, an indigo works, and both a brewery and distillery.

Kershaw's wealth grew steadily. In 1777, as the tumult of the Revolutionary War swirled through the colonies, he took the bold initiative of building a fine home on a high point above the town. Paintings from the 1780s show the house much as it appears today, a graceful two-and-a-half-story home built on an above-ground basement of English brick. Each level featured four rooms, two on each side of a wide center hall, in the style that was popular on both sides of the Atlantic.

In 1780, the British took Charleston and sent a large force inland under the command of Lord Cornwallis. Kershaw and other Camden patriots were vastly outnumbered and chose to surrender. The British immediately took possession of Kershaw's fine new house, building defensive palisades around it. The commanders at the Kershaw house included Cornwallis, Colonel Francis Rawdon, and Banastre "Bloody" Tarleton (who, two hundred years later, would be portrayed as the malevolent British officer in the Mel Gibson movie *The Patriot*). At first, the men of Camden were allowed to move freely, but later, as the American army under General Horatio Gates approached, the British demanded they take up arms against their fellow patriots. Many refused and were jailed. Rawdon thought Kershaw "dangerous" and exiled him to Bermuda until 1782.

The 1780 battle of Camden was a disaster for the patriots, and captured American soldiers were "herded into the backyard [of the Kershaw House] like sheep" to be hung, as one historian noted. A separate legend about the house says that a British officer inside the house was shot by a sharpshooter when he ventured too close to a window.

Joseph Kershaw died in his beloved house in 1794, and the house passed out of the family. For the next sixty years, the house served as a school for an orphan society and later as a private residence. In 1865, Sherman's troops suspected that the house had hidden Confederate munitions and burned it to the ground.

As time passed, the home site became overgrown and then disappeared completely. By the 1940s, no one could quite remember where the old house had once stood. In preparation for the United States' bicentennial, the Camden District Heritage Foundation began archaeological excavations to locate the foundations of the Kershaw house. Historic paintings of the house were studied and funds were raised for reconstruction.

Today, the rebuilt house is externally an exact replica of the original. The interior is modeled on Charleston homes from a similar period. The first floor rooms serve as a museum featuring Georgian-period furnishings. The Kershaw-Cornwallis House is part of Historic Camden, a 107-acre museum and village of buildings that represent the Colonial and Revolutionary periods of the town's past.

FACING PAGE, TOP: KERSHAW-CORNWALLIS HOUSE

FACING PAGE, BOTTOM LEFT: KERSHAW-CORNWALLIS HOUSE, FRONT DOORWAY

FACING PAGE, BOTTOM RIGHT: KERSHAW-CORNWALLIS HOUSE, DETAIL

FLORENCE AREA

The Columns

5001 RANKIN PLANTATION ROAD
FLORENCE, SC 29506

In 1850, Dr. William Rogers Johnson wanted to build a plantation home that would enhance his growing political career. As a doctor, Johnson was known for his research on malaria; as a politician, he served terms in both South Carolina's House and Senate.

It took a team of artisan slaves more than eight years to complete The Columns, which today is considered one of South Carolinas finest examples of Greek Revival architecture. The dominant feature of the house is the overarching hip roof supported by twenty-two towering Doric columns.

Virtually all the materials used in the construction of the house originated from the plantation itself. The lumber came from trees felled and hauled by ox teams to a mill forty-five miles away in Cheraw. The milled lumber was floated by barge back down the Pee Dee River to the house site. The columns are constructed from rounded bricks made from clay found on the land. The bricks were formed, kiln-baked, and set in layers that taper gracefully as they rise. Then they were plastered over to give the columns their smooth façade.

Within the grand house, twelve-foot-high ceilings give the rooms a sense of spaciousness and help keep them cool, while large windows let in light and the summer breezes that stir across the surrounding farmland. There are four comfortable and inviting rooms on the first floor, all opening on the broad central hallway. The gentleman's drawing room and parlor feature extra touches of elegance, including wainscoting, decorative plaster cornices, ceiling medallions, and chandeliers. Upstairs,

88 | SOUTH CAROLINA'S PLANTATIONS & HISTORIC HOMES

there are five bright and airy bedrooms. Floors throughout the house are heart-of-pine.

Behind the home stand several outbuildings, one of which was originally Johnson's apothecary. Another outbuilding was used to generate gas from carbide to fuel the gas lights in the house.

The Columns did not get its name until 1902. That was the year the plantation was bought by Southern lumberman Walter Lacy Rankin for his new bride, Jennie Robertson. It was Jennie who gave the estate its name, and she loved the house and her life there. Tragedy came, however, when Walter was killed in an accident on the farm. Jennie continued to live at The Columns and renamed her daughter Lacy in honor of her husband.

In 1927, Lacy Rankin married Baxter Hicks Harwell in a ceremony that took place in the house. The Columns has remained in the Harwell family since then. In 1938, the home's elegant façade attracted the attention of a Hollywood studio, who used it as a model in the 20th Century Fox movie *Carolina*, starring Robert Young, Janet Gaynor, and six-year-old Shirley Temple.

With more than one thousand acres currently under cultivation, The Columns is one of South Carolina's oldest working plantations. On a summer's day, a regular stream of farm trucks and tractors move between the fields and the outbuildings near the house via a quarter-mile allée of pecan, oak, and sycamore trees. While the house is privately owned, regularly scheduled tours are offered to the public throughout the year.

TOP: THE COLUMNS

INSET: THE COLUMNS

FACING PAGE: THE COLUMNS

Darby Plantation

1150 AUGUSTA ROAD
TRENTON, SC 29847

In 1842, Anne Patience Griffin married a dashing young Edgefield lawyer named Milledge Luke Bonham. Shortly after their wedding, they moved into the tidy house that Anne's father built for them on the Up Country Darby Plantation.

The Darby house is a simple yet graceful Greek Revival home. Its most prominent feature is the deep, wraparound porch whose roof is supported by twelve sturdy pillars. The large double-entry doors flanked with decorative sidelights lead into a wide and inviting central hallway. Ornate hand carving adorns both the doors of the entry hall and the large sliding doors that open from the library and parlor into the hallway, creating a grand space for parties and social functions. In the back of the entry hall, the graceful curved staircase features a broad landing where, according to family legends, musicians would play during balls.

Constructed of traditional pine planking over massive hand-hewn beams, the house features rooms that measure twenty feet square and have twelve-foot-high ceilings that help dissipate the summer heat. The bricks used in the basement and chimneys were hauled to the site by wagon from Augusta, Georgia.

The house was built shortly after Bonham returned from the Second Seminole War, in which he commanded a company of South Carolina Volunteers. He hoped to come back to the quiet life of a planter and attorney, but the quiet did not last. His brother, James, had been killed defending the Alamo in 1836. When war broke out with Mexico, Bonham saw an opportunity to take action and commanded a full Virginia regiment throughout the conflict, rising to the rank of colonel.

Shortly after his return from that conflict, Bonham was elected to the U.S. Congress. At the outbreak of the Civil War, he was appointed commander-in-chief of South Carolina's ten-thousand-man volunteer army. He commanded forces during the First Battle of Bull Run and is said to have been an impressive figure on the battlefield, both respected and liked by officers and enlisted men. Bonham resigned his commission when he was elected governor of South Carolina in 1862.

In 1863, Bonham sold Darby Plantation to George A. Trenholm. During the Civil War, Trenholm's successful cotton company acted as the Confederate government's sole overseas banker, provided financing for arms in exchange for cotton and other goods. Trenholm's ships proved to be wily blockade runners, and he amassed a substantial fortune while supporting the Confederate cause.

Throughout the Civil War, the Darby house was often used as a supply house, holding food and gunpowder for the Confederate army. It also sheltered those escaping the hostilities, including Professor Francis S. Holmes of the Museum of Charleston, who arrived with some of the museum's most valuable collections to be stored in the plantation's outbuildings.

Darby remains a working plantation today. The house sits on a rise, surrounded by shade trees and country gardens and offering a view across extensive fields of cotton and other crops. Darby Plantation has been owned since 1878 by the Wise family, who open their house for tours by reservation.

FACING PAGE, TOP: DARBY PLANTATION

FACING PAGE, BOTTOM: DARBY PLANTATION, GARDEN

INSET: DARBY PLANTATION

EDGEFIELD

Magnolia Dale

320 NORRIS STREET
EDGEFIELD, SC 29824

Magnolia Dale, an elegant townhouse, sits well back from the street on a tree-shaded lot at the edge of historic Edgefield's business district. The house was built in 1843 by Samuel Brooks of Middlesex, Connecticut, on land originally part of a large grant made to Peter Youngblood in 1762.

Brooks lived in Edgefield for thirty years before selling the house and land in 1873 to prominent local businessman and lawyer Alfred Norris and his wife, Mary. The Norrises' daughter, Mamie, was raised at Magnolia Dale and was married there to Jim Tillman, who eventually became lieutenant governor of South Carolina. Tillman was the nephew of South Carolina political firebrand "Pitchfork" Ben Tillman, a U.S. Senator; Pitchfork won his nickname when he gave a public speech declaring he might go to the White House to prod President Grover Cleveland into action with a pitchfork.

Magnolia Dale has changed little since the days of Mamie and Jim Tillman. A long, landscaped walkway leads to the grand portico, which is supported by four imposing columns. The broad hiproof incorporates the portico and shades a small second-floor balcony. One of Magnolia Dale's most interesting features is the outside stairway at the rear of the house, built into an inset porch. The lower floor of the house features a classic four-room design; there are two rooms on each side of a wide hallway that runs from the front to the back of the house. Upstairs, the rooms are less symmetrically laid out, probably because the original four-room design was divided to make additional bedrooms for children and servants.

FACING PAGE: MAGNOLIA DALE

In 1929, the Kendall Company, which owned a large textile mill in Edgefield, bought Magnolia Dale and used portions of the large land parcel to develop a model community for its mill workers. The company also performed substantial restoration work on the house itself and eventually donated it to the town's historical society in 1959. Today, Magnolia Dale is open to the public by appointment.

The house is decorated with period furnishings, mostly from the mid-nineteenth century. One of the prominent portraits hanging in Magnolia Dale's formal parlor is of Arthur Simkins, known as the Father of Edgefield. Simkins was one of many who came from Virginia to the Carolinas seeking better farmlands just before and after the Revolutionary War. He had already established a successful plantation called Cedar Fields on Log Creek. After the local courthouse was built in 1787, Simkins bought a portion of the surrounding land and had it sectioned into streets and lots for Court House Village, which became Edgefield.

Since its founding, Edgefield and the surrounding district have contributed ten governors to South Carolina. Edgefield's best-known politician was Strom Thurmond, who was born in town and died in 2002 at the age of one hundred, after serving in the U.S. Senate for a record forty-eight consecutive years. A second-floor room at Magnolia Dale is devoted to memorabilia, clippings, and photographs that honor Edgefield's most famous native son.

Oakley Park

300 Columbia Road
Edgefield, SC 29824

Oakley Park is one of the most historic homes in one of South Carolina's most historic towns. The home that Daniel Bird built just outside Edgefield in 1835 was a stylish, early Greek Revival dwelling. It had a striking two-story wraparound porch, shaded by an overextending hiproof and supported by nine graceful square pillars. The doors at the front and back of the house are ornate Palladian designs topped by elegant fan lights. Above the main entrance is a small second-floor balcony.

The house itself is a traditional design with four rooms downstairs and four rooms upstairs. Each floor is bisected by spacious hallways. The hallways are separated front and rear by archways intricately carved with delicate magnolia-leaf patterns. The floors throughout the house are heart-of-pine, and the framework includes massive hand-hewn sills that are each fifteen inches square and more than twenty feet long.

The house is best known for its fourth owner, Martin Witherspoon Gary. An outspoken lawyer, Gary was one of South Carolina's most successful cotton planters. Elected to the State House of Representatives in 1860, he was a strong advocate of states' rights. He enthusiastically joined the Confederate Army, fighting with honor in many of the Civil War's key battles. He served longest

under General Wade Hampton, eventually rising to the rank of brigadier general. At Appomattox, he refused to surrender with General Lee; instead, he slipped through enemy lines to meet Confederate President Jefferson Davis, escorting him as far as Cokesbury, South Carolina.

When Gary returned to Edgefield, he took up residence at Oakley Park and continued his life as a cotton planter and lawyer. Along with many residents of South Carolina, he rankled under the federal "Radical Rule" of Reconstruction. He was a leading figure in the formation of the Red Shirts, a citizen's army composed largely of ex-Confederate soldiers whose goal was to return the political control of the South to Southerners, often through violent means. In the hotly contested election of 1876, Gary's old friend and command-ing officer, Wade Hampton, ran for governor. On a summer morning that year, Gary stood on the upper balcony at Oakley Park and addressed 1,500 Red Shirts gathered on the grounds. He extolled them to travel throughout the state and "ensure the vote by any means." Gary's Red Shirts were successful; Hampton was elected, and Reconstruction came to an end. For his part in Hampton's election, Gary won a seat in the State Assembly, but felt he deserved more. He challenged his old friend Hampton politically, which proved disastrous. His political career over, Gary eventually returned to Edgefield a bitter man.

THIS SPREAD: OAKLEY PARK

Today, the house is owned and operated by the United Daughters of the Confederacy and is open to the public. It sits amid pleasant grounds planted with a profusion of magnolias, camellias, azaleas, and live oaks. Behind the house, the original two-room outdoor kitchen still stands. The interior is carefully restored and furnished with mid- to late-nineteenth-century antiques. Many furnishings are from the Gary family, including the formal dining table owned by Governor John Gary Evans, the last Gary to reside at Oakley Park.

NORTH AUGUSTA AREA

Redcliffe Plantation

181 REDCLIFFE ROAD
BEECH ISLAND, SC 29842

In 1855, James Henry Hammond wrote to a friend, "I purchased not long ago Dr. Milledge Galphin's residence in Beech Island and named it Redcliffe from the red bluff in front of it. . . . It is a beautiful situation, susceptible to magnificent improvements and has the finest view in the middle country."

A severe drought delayed Hammond's "magnificent improvements," but in 1857 he started work on an elegant new home that he had been planning for years. He was only two weeks into the project when he was elected to the U.S. Senate and had to leave the construction under the management of his son, Harry.

By the time Hammond returned from Washington, D.C., the house was complete. The construction had cost him the princely sum of $22,000, but as he entered Redcliffe's grounds he was delighted with what he saw. The house sat like an exquisite wedding cake atop a gentle rise of land, which gave it an unrestricted view across the mighty Savannah River to the rooftops of Augusta, Georgia, five miles away. An elegant Georgian-style celebration of symmetry, the exterior of the house featured perfectly balanced placement of doors and windows.

FACING PAGE: REDCLIFFE PLANTATION

On each of the four sides, eleven-foot-high single doors opened onto two-tiered porches that were supported by elegantly tapered Corinthian columns.

The Redcliffe house was constructed from materials originating on the property as well as from suppliers in Augusta. Some of the lumber came from the plantation's forests, including the sycamore used as banisters, library bookcases, and doors (which were hung on silver-plated hinges). The house had two main floors plus an attic. It was originally built on immense brick piers, which were later replaced by a full basement when the house was found to be difficult to heat. The main floor follows a four-room plan; each room measures twenty by twenty-six feet, and the full-length central hallway is an amazing twenty feet wide. The rooms have fourteen-foot-high ceilings and ornate plasterwork highlighted by decorative medallions and cornices.

Redcliffe was never meant to be a working plantation in the traditional sense; instead it was a gentleman's farm, where Hammond enjoyed a tranquil retreat from the demands of public office. Here, he dedicated himself to his true love, horticultural research. The four hundred acres surrounding the house were a wonderland of flowering trees and shrubs, extensive orchards, a vineyard, and acres of unique and unusual plantings. Hammond published his agricultural findings often and was a founding member of the notable Beech Island Agricultural Society.

An ardent secessionist and admirer of John C. Calhoun, Hammond served terms in the U.S. House of Representatives, the Senate, and a brief term as governor of South Carolina. He was a complex man and even his friends often considered him brash and arrogant. He publicly admitted

marrying his wife for her money. His career was constantly hampered by scandals of his own making, and his wife finally left him after discovering his ongoing affairs with two slaves. During the Civil War, Hammond was bitterly disappointed by the Confederate Army losses suffered. He died of stomach ailments in 1864, just before the Union Army arrived to take control of the region.

Known as "Harry" to his friends, Hammond's son, Henry, served as a Confederate officer and surrendered at Appomattox with Lee. Harry returned to Redcliffe with "a pipe, some tobacco and literally nothing else." Through dedication and hard work, he managed to hold on to Redcliffe in the difficult years after the war. During Harry's ownership, the house's porches were removed and replaced with single-story wraparound porches. In 1901, Harry had the badly deteriorated rooftop observatory removed, replacing it with a simple widow's walk. Harry died at Redcliffe Plantation in 1916, and during the next twenty years the house fell deeply into disrepair.

The last Hammond descendant to occupy Redcliffe was John Shaw Billings II, who had been born in the house and felt that it needed to be preserved. A successful journalist, he had worked his way up to become editor of *Time* and later *Life* magazines. In 1954, he moved to Redcliffe and began a long-overdue renovation of the house. In 1975, he gifted Redcliffe to the State of South Carolina, which operates it today as a state park.

The park service has begun to reestablish the great landscape created by James Henry Hammond in the 1850s. Visitors enter the grounds along a mile-long allée of mature magnolias. The grounds around the house are dotted with exotic trees, such as Spanish cork oak, Chinese pistachio, and Chinese parasol—all remnants of James Hammond's "magnificent improvements."

FACING PAGE: REDCLIFFE PLANTATION, PORCH

ABOVE: REDCLIFFE PLANTATION, STABLES

LEFT: REDCLIFFE PLANTATION, DETAIL

BRATTONSVILLE

Brattonsville Homestead House

1444 BRATTONSVILLE ROAD
McCONNELS, SC 29726

The Homestead House is one of several well-preserved homes and buildings that make up the historic settlement of Brattonsville. Each of the homes at Brattonsville reflects a different generation of the Bratton family dynasty, which started humbly in pre-Revolutionary times and grew to be a dominant force in South Carolina.

The Brattonsville story began with Colonel William Bratton, a Revolutionary War officer. Bratton was one of the militia commanders at the Battle of Huck's Defeat, a local battle that gave the patriots a small but psychologically important victory and was considered a key turning point in the war. Part of a group of Scots-Irish settlers who arrived in the colonies in the 1740s, Bratton started with just two hundred acres. Realizing the importance of his homestead's crossroad location, he started a tavern in the lower rooms of his house. Later, he purchased an early cotton gin and acquired slaves to put his fields into cotton.

The homestead was built by Bratton's youngest son, John, whose talents as both merchant and planter brought Brattonsville into its own. Under John's management, the plantation came to encompass more than six thousand acres, and the commercial endeavors grew to include a saw mill, brick kiln, blacksmith, and country store. He also started a successful academy for young women around 1840.

The Homestead House is an excellent example of an early-nineteenth-century Up Country plantation house. Built in 1823, the first completed version was a Federal-style four-over-four with a central hall, interior chimneys, and Robert Adams–style fireplace mantles. The Greek Revival side wings were added in 1826; the Greek style was further enhanced by the two-story piazza added in 1854. The house's simple elegance attracted the attention of Hollywood, where the home served as a prominent set for the Mel Gibson Revolutionary War movie, *The Patriot*.

One of The Homestead House's most impressive features is the large, detached formal dining room, which is reached via a breezeway attached to the house. This imposing room is one of the few such detached dining rooms in the United States. Measuring more than forty feet long by twenty feet wide with a twelve-foot-high ceiling, it was used by the Brattons for formal dinners, parties, recitals, and dances. The room features large windows that admit welcome breezes in hot weather. A pianoforte dating to 1845 recalls the days when the room was used as a gathering place for students in the women's academy. On the far wall, built-in storage closets around the large fireplace once held the dishes, silver, and serving utensils required for large-scale entertaining.

FACING PAGE, TOP:
BRATTONSVILLE
HOMESTEAD HOUSE

FACING PAGE, BOTTOM:
BRATTONSVILLE HOMESTEAD
HOUSE, DEPENDENCY

The Homestead House and other historic buildings at Historic Brattonsville are open daily for tours. The house contains furnishings from the late eighteenth to the mid-nineteenth centuries. Several pieces are original to the Bratton family, including the sofa and the cellaret located in the formal parlor. Behind the house, a detached kitchen has been reconstructed on the foundations of the original building. There are also two brick slave houses, which were home to some of the 140 slaves that Dr. John Bratton owned at the time of his death.

ABOVE: BRATTONSVILLE HOMESTEAD HOUSE, FORMAL DINING ROOM

FACING PAGE, BOTTOM: BRATTONSVILLE HOMESTEAD HOUSE, SMOKEHOUSE

FACING PAGE, BOTTOM: BRATTONSVILLE HOMESTEAD HOUSE, PARLOR

Part III
PIEDMONT PLANTATIONS
& HISTORIC HOMES

UNION AREA

Rose Hill Plantation

2677 SARDIS ROAD
UNION, SC 29379

The house at Rose Hill Plantation is one of South Carolina's best examples of a Federal-style home that was renovated in the 1850s to the then-modern Greek Revival style. The original house was built in 1832 by William Henry Gist. A classic four-over-four Federal-style house, it featured an all-brick façade, exterior chimneys at each end, and a wood-shingle roof.

The Federal style incorporated simple lines and symmetry, but by the 1850s it was considered outdated. The newer Greek Revival style, championed first in England, then brought across the Atlantic, was felt to represent the highest ideals of humankind. It also conveniently lent itself to displaying the newfound wealth of a rapidly growing nation.

Around 1850, Gist and his wife, Mary, began a major renovation of their home. They added porticos on three sides. The front and rear porticos were two stories tall and topped by pediments; they had graceful columns supporting wrought-iron railed balconies at the second floor. Pediments were also added to the gable ends of the house. The exterior walls were covered with stucco, primarily for decorative purposes, but also to waterproof the brick. Lastly, the oak-shingle roof was replaced with tin.

Today, the Rose Hill house is surrounded by the dense woodlands of Sumter National Forest, but in the 1840s, the cultivated land of numerous plantations stretched along the banks of the Tyger River and across the surrounding rolling terrain. Rose Hill, like its neighbors, was an Up Country plantation that grew hardy, short-fiber Upland cotton, as well as raising cattle and growing all the produce the local populace required.

When Gist was elected governor of South Carolina in 1858, the Rose Hill house became the governor's mansion. Gist was the last governor to undertake his duties from his personal residence. Politically, he was an avid secessionist and made throwing off the mantle of the federal government the central theme of his term. At one point, he sent his cousin and trusted aide, States Rights Gist (yes, his given name really was States Rights, proving that William Gist was not the family's only ardent secessionist) to other surrounding Southern states offering support should they vote to secede.

When Abraham Lincoln was elected president, it provided just the ammunition William Gist was looking for, and he called a special meeting of the State Assembly to draft South Carolina's response. On December 20, 1860, five days after Gist's term ended, South Carolina officially announced its secession from the United States.

Gist continued to live at the Rose Hill house until his death in 1874. In the twentieth century, the house fell into disrepair, and in 1940 it was slated to become a bombing target for planes from nearby Shaw Air Force Base. Last-minute work on the part of local preservationists kept the house from this fate.

Today, Rose Hill is operated as a state park open to the public. The house has been fully renovated and furnished with period antiques, including many objects from the Gist family and several once actually owned by William and Mary.

TOP: ROSE HILL PLANTATION

INSET: ROSE HILL PLANTATION, GARDENS

FOLLOWING PAGES: ROSE HILL PLANTATION

AND ROSE HILL PLANTATION, GARDENS

ABBEVILLE

Burt-Stark Mansion

400 NORTH MAIN STREET
ABBEVILLE, SC 29620

If historians were called on to pick a moment that signaled the fall of the Confederacy, they would likely choose the afternoon of May 2, 1865, when Confederate President Jefferson Davis held his final cabinet meeting in the front parlor of the Burt-Stark Mansion.

The story of the Burt-Stark Mansion begins in the 1840s with Abbeville lawyer and planter David Lesley and an extraordinarily talented slave named Cubic. Legend has it that Lesley's Northern-born wife admired a particular house in the Hudson Valley of New York state. Lesley sent Cubic to New York to study the house and then recreate it in Abbeville. Leading a team of skilled carpenters and craftsmen who were probably all slaves, Cubic took more than ten years to complete the building.

ABOVE: BURT-STARK MANSION

FACING PAGE: BURT-STARK MANSION

The result is the Burt-Stark Mansion, an excellent example of Greek Revival architecture. Four imposing pillars support a massive pediment atop the two-story portico, which dominates the mansion's front façade. The front of the house retains classical symmetry, but the left side features a second façade, less severe and almost Victorian, and a welcoming shady porch defined by decorative wrought-iron balustrades. The interior of the house speaks of the many generations of affluent owners. The two front parlors and hallway could, in the house's glory days, be opened into one large space for dances and entertaining. The house has been fully furnished with antebellum antiques, and the front parlor has been decorated much as it would have been during Jefferson Davis's final cabinet meeting.

Lesley died in 1855, and in 1862, the property was purchased by Armistead Burt, who had served in the U.S. House of Representatives from 1843 to 1852. His wife, Martha Calhoun Burt, was a niece of the legendary politician and orator John C. Calhoun. Martha was responsible for one of house's most interesting decorative features, the fan-shaped stained-glass transom located above the entry hall divider, whose design honors her French Huguenot heritage.

During Burt's second session of Congress, he befriended a fellow representative named Jefferson Davis, who would go on to become the president of the Confederate States and the most famous guest of the mansion. On April 16, 1865, Davis's wife, Verina, and her children, arrived in Abbeville after fleeing the fall of Richmond. With them was a troop of handpicked soldiers guarding the remaining gold of the Confederate treasury. Her husband's old friend, Armistead Burt, offered her a place to stay. When she warned him that Union troops might burn his house for harboring her, Burt reportedly responded, "Madam, I know of no finer use my house could be put to than to be burned for such a cause."

Verina continued south, ironically leaving just a few days before her husband and several of his senior cabinet members, generals, and officers arrived in Abbeville on May 2. They too were welcomed by Burt, who offered Davis the same room his wife had used just days before.

Although the Union army was pursuing him, Davis was staunchly confident that if he could reach the remaining Confederate armies to the south and west, there was yet hope for the Southern cause. At 4:00 p.m. in the front parlor, he convened what was to be the final meeting of his cabinet. There, in spite of Davis's resolve, his cabinet ministers and trusted generals dashed any hopes he had by unanimously rejecting his plans for continuing the war. The Confederate soldiers, the generals told Davis, "would fight bravely to ensure his safe escape, but not fire another shot to prolong the war." In shock and dismay, Davis slumped, saying, "Then all is truly lost." The Confederacy's secretary of war, General John C. Breckenridge, urged Davis to flee, and at midnight, the entourage left the Abbeville mansion.

FACING PAGE: BURT-STARK
MANSION, FRONT DOORWAY

In the aftermath of the Civil War, the Burt family lost much of their wealth; in 1868, they were forced to sell their home. The house went through a succession of owners until it was purchased by the Stark family in 1900.

Anne Miller Stark, who was a niece of Martha Burt, lovingly restored the house. Her daughter, Mary Stark Davis, willed the house to "a properly formed public body" in 1971. She continued to live in the house until her death in 1987 at the age of 102. Just prior to her death, legend has it she warned that on "Judgment Day" she would return through the front door—"and you better not have moved anything." To this day "Miss Mary's" slippers lie at her bed, her dress hangs nearby, and little in the house has changed to raise her wrath should she return.

SPARTANBURG AREA

Price House

1200 OAK VIEW FARM ROAD
WOODRUFF, SC 29367

Thomas Price was already a successful merchant when he moved to the Spartanburg District with his wife, Anne. The land he purchased in 1794 was located on the Spartanburg–Cross Anchor stagecoach line and, seizing an opportunity, he obtained a license "to sell spirituous liquors and keep a publick house of entertainment," the common term for a tavern or stagecoach stop.

The house he built in 1795 featured a high gambrel roof and eighteen-inch-thick brick walls laid in an elaborate Flemish bond. The design was unusual for the Carolina Up Country and had more in common with houses of that period found in Maryland and along the Chesapeake Bay.

Price was a man who wore many hats. In addition to running his tavern, he operated a general store. He also served as postmaster and operated a post office from 1811 to 1820. His lands included some two thousand acres that he farmed with the help of more than twenty-four slaves.

In the raw wilderness of the Carolina Up Country in 1795, the unusual, imposing design of the Price House spoke of wealth and privilege. The downstairs features a simple but spacious two-room design. The dining room is large, designed to serve not only the family but also hungry stagecoach travelers. The parlor is referred to as the Pine Room for the full-length pine paneling that decorates it. The paneling is original to the house and was cut from trees on the property at the time the house was built.

FACING PAGE: PRICE HOUSE

The second floor features two large bedrooms and a third smaller room tucked in between, which was likely used for visiting children or relatives, as the Prices had no children of their own. The third floor includes two bedrooms tucked under the eaves; these were rooms for overnight stagecoach guests, one for women, one for men. There may have only been one or two beds per room, and often travelers had to share their bed with strangers.

An archaeological excavation in 1970 confirmed that numerous outbuildings once stood on the grounds, including the general store and post office, a smokehouse, slave quarters, and the kitchen. Beneath the kitchen was a cold cellar, where dairy products and other perishables would have been stored to keep them cool. The foundation of the kiln where the house's bricks were baked is believed to be located nearby, on private property.

Thomas Price died in 1820, and the rear addition of the house is thought to have been built shortly thereafter, probably as accommodation for servants. When Anne passed away in 1821, she left a forty-two-page inventory of the estate, including all of the goods in the house.

The Spartanburg County Historical Association acquired the property in 1968 and used Anne's extensive inventory to recreate the Price's furnishings and decor. The house is open for tours on weekends and by reservation.

Walnut Grove Plantation

1200 OTTS SHOALS ROAD
ROEBUCK, SC 29376

For Charles and Mary Moore, it was a long road from northern Ireland to the placid rolling hills of South Carolina's Up Country. Like thousands of Scots-Irish immigrants before them, they arrived first in Philadelphia. Finding good farmland expensive, they headed south along the Great Wagon Road, seeking open land in the largely unsettled Up Country of South Carolina. The road they followed for more than six hundred miles was little more than a rough path that led through the mountains, becoming ever more rugged and undeveloped on its southward journey. When Charles Moore arrived in 1763, he carried a land grant from King George III for 550 acres near present-day Spartanburg. Once on the land, he set about building a home for himself and his family at the edge of the American frontier.

The Moores were relatively affluent, and the house they built was sophisticated by the standards of the day. The construction was of logs, dovetailed at the corners. But unlike many of their neighbors'

one-room, mud-chinked log cabins, their house was two full stories and sheathed in pine clapboards. Inside, the walls had wood paneling, and every room boasted glass windows.

The first floor contained the large central "keeping room," where most of the activities of daily life occurred, as well as the Moores' bedroom. Upstairs was originally one large room where the children slept, but that room was later partitioned off, perhaps to create separate rooms for the children as they grew older. Later, the rear porch was enclosed to create a dining room and changing room where food brought from the outside kitchen was transferred from pots to dishes. The large wraparound porch offered cooling shade in the summer heat and was part of the original construction.

The Moores had ten children, several of whom came of age at the height of the Revolutionary War. The oldest daughter, Kate, was married to patriot officer Captain Andrew Barry. Family records indicate that Kate spied both for her husband and for General Daniel Morgan, who led the patriot forces to victory at the nearby Battle of Cowpens.

In 1780, Walnut Grove was the stage for a bloody chapter in the war. One day an ailing patriot officer, Captain Ben Steadman, was recuperating in the house and two soldiers were visiting him. They heard horses coming down the road in front of the house and were alarmed to see 250 Tory soldiers approaching, led by British officer "Bloody" Bill Cunningham. The British had learned that Steadman was in the area and were searching for him. Kate Moore heard the commotion and raced to alert patriot forces in the area. The Tories shot down the two visiting patriot soldiers as they fled into the woods and later killed Captain Steadman. Their plans to burn the house were cut short, however, by the arrival of Captain Andrew Barry and his patriot forces, who skirmished with the Tories and forced them to withdraw.

Through hard work and perseverance, the Moores increased their landholdings to more than three thousand acres. Charles and Mary lived long lives, and both were in their seventies when they died in 1805.

The house remained remarkably unchanged over the next century and a half. The Moores' descendants gave it to the Spartanburg County Historical Association in 1961, and after six years of restoration it was opened to the public as a historic house museum in 1967.

Today, the property still has many outbuildings like the ones that were part of the Colonial-era plantation, including a barn, blacksmith forge, wheat house, and dry cellar. Inside the house, over the doorway to the changing room, hangs a musket. It was a gift from Amanda Blake who played Kitty in the long-running TV western series *Gunsmoke*. She is just one of many descendants of Charles and Mary Moore, who so long ago built this small house at the edge of the vast American wilderness.

FACING PAGE, TOP: WALNUT GROVE PLANTATION

FACING PAGE, INSET: WALNUT GROVE PLANTATION

ABOVE, LEFT: WALNUT GROVE PLANTATION, KITCHEN

ABOVE, RIGHT: WALNUT GROVE PLANTATION, BARN

CLEMSON & PENDLETON AREA

Ashtabula Plantation

444 HIGHWAY 88
PENDLETON, SC 29670

Ashtabula's story begins around 1790, when Thomas Lofton received 320 acres of land in return for his service as sheriff. He built a modest two-story brick dwelling that is still standing and that served as the dependency, or out building, for the current plantation house.

That plantation house was begun in 1825 by Lewis Ladson Gibbes, who built a frame, two-over-two, traditional Up Country farmhouse in front of Lofton's original brick house. Gibbes, originally from Charleston, developed a self-sustaining farm and increased the size of the plantation to about six hundred acres. Little is known of Gibbes, but his wife, Maria Drayton Gibbes, was an avid botanist and naturalist. She raised their son, Lewis Reeves Gibbes, to love nature and the outdoors. He became a prominent botanist himself and was an associate of famed naturalist and ornithologist James Audubon.

By the economic boom of the 1850s, Ashtabula had become one of the finest plantations nestled along the fertile banks of Eighteen Mile Creek. The plantation lands had expanded to more than twelve hundred acres, and the frame house was enlarged to its current, traditional, four-over-four room design.

The plantation house's most striking feature is its wraparound porch, which offers cooling views across a broad lawn that is shaded by large oaks and other hardwoods. The porch roof is supported by sturdy pillars, and the porch ceiling is painted sky blue, which was popular on antebellum porches. On the east side, a modern patio connects the main house to the 1790 brick dependency, which at various times has served as the plantation office, servants' quarters, kitchen, and a guesthouse.

FACING PAGE: ASHTABULA PLANTATION

ABOVE: ASHTABULA PLANTATION, DINING ROOM

Inside the main house, the rooms are spacious, yet maintain an inviting warmth. As an Up Country plantation, Ashtabula was first and foremost a hard-working farm. Yet the families that built and expanded Ashtabula found subtle ways to display their growing wealth. The decorated cast-iron fireplace surrounds and fine wallpaper in the front parlor both are good examples, as these type of things are found only in the houses of the most prosperous planters.

During the Civil War, the plantation was owned by Clarissa Adger Bowen and her husband, O. A. Bowen. Throughout the war, Clarissa kept a journal that detailed the war's affect on small towns and farms in the Up Country. Just as important, she captured wonderful details about everyday life on a nineteenth-century South Carolina plantation. The journal has been published, and the perfect place to peruse it is on Ashtabula's porch. Here it is easy to imagine Clarissa's world, perhaps a Sunday afternoon, when guests would drop by on their return from church. The men would talk politics, cotton, and cattle; the women would serve sweet tea and share news of children, projects, and social events. It is a past that seems to linger in the shady peacefulness of Ashtabula Plantation.

Today, the Ashtabula house is owned and operated as a museum by the Pendleton Historic Foundation. Most of the furniture is authentic to the 1850s, when the house was completed. In the master bedroom, the canopy bed is itself a victim of the Civil War. Careful observation will reveal a mini-ball buried in the wood of the post, purportedly lodged there during the Battle of Columbia.

FACING PAGE, TOP: ASHTABULA PLANTATION, DRAWING ROOM

FACING PAGE, BOTTOM: ASHTABULA PLANTATION, MASTER BEDROOM

TOP AND LEFT: ASHTABULA PLANTATION, ORIGINAL DWELLING

Fort Hill

CALHOUN DRIVE
CLEMSON, SC 29634

Standing serenely amid the modern buildings of Clemson University, Fort Hill is best known as the home of South Carolina's most eminent politician and famed orator, John C. Calhoun. Calhoun acquired the property in 1825 and lived there until his death in 1850.

The property's original house, called Clergy Hall, was built in 1803 by Dr. James McElhenny. During the two and a half decades Calhoun resided in the building, Calhoun made several additions, including the elegant Greek Revival porticos that grace the north, east, and south sides of the house.

Calhoun renamed his estate Fort Hill in honor of a wooden fort that was built nearby in 1776 for defense against Indians. The house eventually grew to include fourteen rooms, each with its own fireplace. Downstairs, the ornate formal parlor, with its low-key décor of red, white, and blue, and the large state dining room speak of Calhoun's positions both as a political leader and the head of a large family.

The rambling upstairs includes eight bedrooms, which were likely added and subdivided as Calhoun's family grew. All of the rooms are furnished with period pieces, many of which can be

traced to the Calhoun family. Some of the most interesting of these are the desks and office furnishings found in Calhoun's private office, which stands directly behind the house. In this private retreat, Calhoun met with political leaders from around the nation and forged many of the relationships that nurtured his political career.

Calhoun considered Fort Hill to be his oasis of peace during his turbulent political career. A Phi Beta Kappa graduate of Yale, Calhoun served in the South Carolina State Assembly and the House of Representatives, earning a reputation as a fair but fiery politician and a brilliant debater. As a U.S. senator for South Carolina, he formed the famed triumvirate of classic American orators with Daniel Webster and Henry Clay. He also served as vice president under two presidents, John Quincy Adams and Andrew Jackson.

FACING PAGE, INSET: FORT HILL, JOHN C. CALHOUN OFFICE

FACING PAGE, BOTTOM AND ABOVE: FORT HILL

It has been said that Calhoun was the prime architect of the South's secession and the tragedy of the Civil War. Calhoun, however, believed that his vehement defense of states' rights and the institution of slavery were in the interest of preserving the Union, for he felt that if the Southern states were forced to surrender these institutions, they would surely secede. Calhoun died in 1850, feeling defeated and predicting the division of the Union was inevitable. America, however, honored him. In Washington, his body lay in state in the Senate chambers, public buildings were draped with emblems of mourning, and flags flew at half-staff.

Fort Hill passed to Calhoun's daughter, Anna, who in turn left it to her husband, Thomas Clemson, with the understanding that the land be used for the creation of "a school as a fitting memorial to the Calhoun and Clemson names." Accordingly, the eleven hundred acres of plantation holdings became the grounds of Clemson University, which is consistently ranked among America's top public universities. Clemson University now owns and manages Fort Hill, offering daily tours.

Hanover House

CLEMSON UNIVERSITY
CLEMSON, SC 29634

Almost three hundred years ago, Paul de St. Julien walked the banks of the Cooper River to select a house site for himself and his wife, Mary Aime Ravenel. The site he chose was a good one, located on a high bluff of the river, near a primitive road called Charichy Path, assuring his estate would be linked by both land and water to the thriving port of Charleston.

Paul de St. Julien was the grandson of Pierre St. Julien de Malacare, who was a wealthy Huguenot and one of more than five hundred thousand Huguenots displaced by religious persecution in Europe. Many escaped to England where, as Protestants, they gained the favor of King George I, Elector of Hanover; King George granted them title to lands in South Carolina where they could

THIS SPREAD: HANOVER HOUSE settle. It was in the king's honor that Paul named his estate and house Hanover.

In 1714, the land was still raw frontier, and the house had to serve not only as home, but also as a business place and wilderness fortress against Indian uprisings. The Tuscarora War had just ended, yet 1715 would witness a violent uprising among the Yemassee and the massacre of more than one hundred Low Country settlers. That uprising may explain why it took two years for St. Julien to complete his "big little house." When he laid the bricks at the top of one chimney, he inscribed the words *Peu a peu* from the French saying "Little by little, the bird builds its nest."

By rural Colonial standards, the house is elegant and elaborate. The foundation is two feet thick, enclosing a basement that originally housed a kitchen and features a storage room with narrow, shuttered gun slots for defending the home. The walls of the house are timber-framed and sheathed with cypress siding. The Gallic gable-style roof is covered with cedar shingles and features small but refined dormers.

From the outside, the house's small appearance is deceptive. Inside, the rooms are spacious, particularly the front parlor, whose massive fireplace and twelve-foot-high ceilings made it comfortable and inviting for family gatherings and entertaining. Below the narrow stairs that lead to the four second-floor bedchambers is a side room that was probably used as an office by St. Julien. Here he conducted the daily business of his expanding plantation.

Through the hundred and fifty years of ownership by the St. Julien family, the house remained remarkably unchanged. One threat Paul de St. Julien could not have foreseen, however, was the damming of the Cooper River for hydroelectricity. By 1930, the house, which stood in the flood zone of the proposed dam, was abandoned and in near-derelict condition.

Hanover House's historic value was recognized by several groups, however. In 1941, Clemson University agreed to relocate and refurbish the home. It was moved onto the university campus, and for the next two decades, various departments of the university undertook a comprehensive restoration. In 1994, it was moved to the university's botanical gardens, where it is open to the public as a museum.

Woodburn Plantation

Woodburn was originally built around 1830 as a "gentleman's farm." Although the estate land was used for agriculture, its main purpose was to serve as an Up Country summer retreat for its first owner, Charles Cotesworth Pinckney.

In the 1800s, the Up Country offered a vastly preferable climate to the Low Country, where summers could be exceedingly hot and humid and where marshes were breeding grounds for malaria-spreading mosquitoes. The Woodburn house was built to take maximum advantage of the Up Country climate.

The house's most imposing feature is the grand, two-story pillared porch that wraps around three sides of the house. The wide verandas made inviting places for the family to sit, take tea, and enjoy the summer breezes. Inside the house, all the main rooms feature large windows and connecting doors, which create maximum ventilation throughout the house. The first floor features a classic four-room layout that offers a pleasing feeling of spaciousness. The house's main entrance is an unusual double stairway; each set of steps leads to French doors that open into the east drawing room and the parlor, respectively.

INSET: WOODBURN PLANTATION

FACING PAGE, TOP:
WOODBURN PLANTATION

FACING PAGE, BOTTOM:
WOODBURN PLANTATION,
PARLOR

The house's prominent porches create the illusion that this is only a two-story home. But there is also a third floor with bedrooms originally used by servants and children, as well as a full basement with a warming kitchen, storage space, and a dining space that provided a cool spot for the family to gather on the hottest summer days.

The house's builder, Charles Pinckney, was born into one of South Carolina's most prominent families. He was the grandson of Eliza Pinckney, who had been instrumental in introducing indigo as a cash crop to the state. His father, Thomas Pinckney, was the governor of South Carolina at the time of Charles's birth and later served as minister to England. His uncle, Charles Cotesworth, for whom he was named, was one of the authors of the U.S. Constitution and twice ran for president.

Known by friends and family as "Cotesworth," Charles Pinckney graduated from Harvard with a law degree and served as lieutenant governor of South Carolina. Still, he preferred the quiet life at Woodburn. Here, he read, continued his families' research into agricultural advances, and worked to promote the religious education of slaves, who were forbidden by law to learn reading or writing.

In the 1850s, Woodburn passed to the Adger family, who occupied the plantation for more than fifty years. During the Civil War, the house often sheltered members of the family who were fleeing embattled parts of the state.

Woodburn hit its peak when the property passed to one of the Adgers' nephews, Major Augustine Smythe. Smythe and his family adored Woodburn, and turned it into a superb stock farm renowned for raising fine horses and prize cattle. One of Smythe's children, Susan Smythe Bennet, wrote in her diary, "I think I loved Woodburn more than any place, anywhere."

Today, the Pendleton Historic Foundation owns the Woodburn house and operates it as a museum, open to the public for tours.

BIBLIOGRAPHY

Brewster, Lawrence Fay. *Summer Migrations and Resorts of South Carolina Low-country Planters.* New York: AMS Press, 1947.

Davis, Evangeline. *Charleston: Houses & Gardens.* Charleston, S.C.: Preservation Society of Charleston, 1975.

Edgar, Walter B. *South Carolina: A History.* Columbia: University of South Carolina Press, 1998.

Hilton, Mary Kendall. *Old Homes & Churches of Beaufort County, South Carolina.* Columbia, S.C.: State Printing Co., 1970.

Historic Resources of the Lowcountry: A Regional Survey of Beaufort County, S.C., Colleton County, S.C., Hampton County S.C., Jasper County, S.C. Yemassee, S.C.: Lowcountry Council of Governments, 1979.

Irving, John B. *A Day on Cooper River.* Enlarged and edited by Louisa Cheves Stoney; reprinted with notes by Samuel Gaillard Stoney. Columbia, S.C.: Press of the R. L. Bryan Company, 1969.

Iseley, N. Jane. *Plantations of the Low Country: South Carolina, 1697–1865.* Greensboro, N.C.: Legacy Publications, 1985.

Lachicotte, Alberta Morel. *Georgetown Rice Plantations.* Columbia, S.C.: State Commercial Printing Co., 1955.

Lane, Mills. *Architecture of the Old South.* New York: Abbeville Press, 1989.

Leiding, Harriette Kershaw. *Historic Houses of South Carolina.* Philadelphia and London: J.B. Lippincott Company, 1921.

Linder, Suzanne Cameron. *Historical Atlas of the Rice Plantations of the ACE River Basin—1860.* Columbia, S.C.: South Carolina Department of Archives & History for the Archives and History Foundation, Ducks Unlimited, and the Nature Conservancy, 1995.

Linder, Suzanne Cameron. *Historical Atlas of the Rice Plantations of Georgetown County and the Santee River.* Columbia, S.C.: South Carolina Department of Archives and History for the Historic Ricefields Association Inc., n.d.

Miner, Robert G., ed. *Colonial Homes in the Southern States.* New York: Arno Press, 1977.

Stockton, Robert P. *Historic Resources of Berkeley County, South Carolina.* N.p.: Preservation Consultants, Inc., 1990.

Stoney, Samuel Gaillard. *Plantations of the Carolina Low Country.* Charleston, S.C.: Carolina Art Association, 1977.

Stuart, Jozefa, and Wilson Randolph Gathings. *Great Southern Mansions.* New York: Walker, 1977.

FACING PAGE, TOP:
WOODBURN PLANTATION, BEDROOM

FACING PAGE, BOTTOM:
WOODBURN PLANTATION, DRAWING ROOM

ABOUT THE AUTHORS

Paul Franklin is a travel photographer and writer whose work has appeared in numerous national publications including *Yankee*, *WoodenBoat*, *Travel America*, *Coast to Coast*, *Harrowsmith*, and others. He recently photographed *Our Washington, D.C.* from Voyageur Press. He is also the author of *The Barnes and Noble Complete Guide to the Public Parks and Gardens of Washington, D.C.*, the Eyewitness Travel Guides *Canada* and *Southwest USA & Las Vegas*, and the *AAA Spiral Guide to Washington, D.C.* He is a member of the American Society of Media Photographers and the American Society of Travel Writers.

Author and researcher Nancy Mikula has a passion for exploring backroads and discovering little-known historic sites. Her articles on travel, historic, and human-interest subjects have appeared in numerous magazines in the U.S and Canada, including *Maturity*, *Leisureways*, and *Writer's Digest*. She recently authored the *Top Ten Guide to Santa Fe and Taos* and is co-author of several books, including the Eyewitness Travel Guide *Arizona & the Grand Canyon*. She spends her winters enjoying the warmth of coastal South Carolina.